T0031661

estherpress

Books for Courageous Women

ESTHER PRESS VISION

Publishing diverse voices that encourage and equip women to walk courageously in the light of God's truth for such a time as this.

BIBLICAL STATEMENT OF PURPOSE

"For if you keep silent at this time, relief and deliverance will rise for the Jews from another place, but you and your father's house will perish. And who knows whether you have not come to the kingdom for such a time as this?"

Esther 4:14 (ESV)

Warrior of Eden

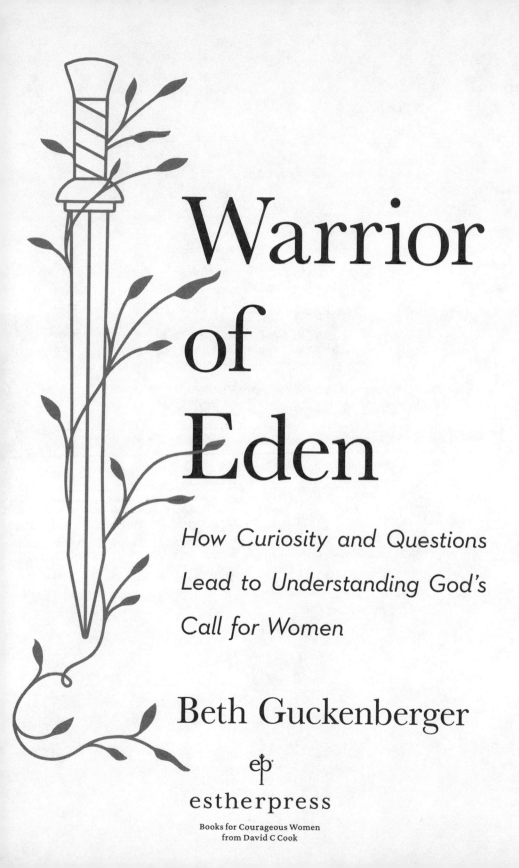

Warrior
of
Eden

*How Curiosity and Questions
Lead to Understanding God's
Call for Women*

Beth Guckenberger

eṗ

estherpress

Books for Courageous Women
from David C Cook

WARRIOR OF EDEN
Published by Esther Press
an imprint of David C Cook
4050 Lee Vance Drive
Colorado Springs, CO 80918 U.S.A.

Integrity Music Limited, a Division of David C Cook
Brighton, East Sussex BN1 2RE, England

The website addresses recommended throughout this book are offered as a resource
to you. These websites are not intended in any way to be or imply an endorsement
on the part of David C Cook, nor do we vouch for their content.

Details in some stories have been changed to protect the identities of the persons involved.

Bible credits are listed at the end of the book.

Library of Congress Control Number 2023940013
ISBN 978-0-8307-8259-8
eISBN 978-0-8307-8261-1

The Team: Michael Covington, Stephanie Bennett, James Hershberger, Jack Campbell, Susan Murdock
Cover Design: Emily Weigel

Printed in the United States of America
First Edition 2024

1 2 3 4 5 6 7 8 9 10

092223

To my mom,
You were the first ezer I saw, and I've been
leaning in to learn from you ever since.

To my daughters,
Watching you engage wholeheartedly in this
world is my greatest joy. Tag, you're it.

To my granddaughters,
Remember the rock from which you were cut and
the quarry from which you were hewn.
Isaiah 51:1

Contents

The Spark That Lit a Fire

I was walking on a dusty trail in Israel, talking to my guide about the Hebrew language. To me, Hebrew words are like doorknobs: when turned, they take you into a new room of understanding.

She said, "I have one for you. Do you know what *ezer* means?"

I shook my head, sensing something good was coming.

She continued, "We see it used almost two dozen times in the Old Testament, but you will be familiar with it in Genesis 2, where it says, 'It's not good for man to be alone, so God created a ...'"

She trailed off, wanting me to finish the sentence.

"... helper suitable for him," I finished.

"Exactly. *Ezer* is translated in English as 'helper.' But that's not the best translation for ezer. Want to know a closer definition?" She stopped hiking and looked at me, assessing if I was ready? Interested? I am not sure, but it felt like I was being evaluated.

"Sure," I answered, already pulling my notebook out. I didn't have to write down what came next because I will never forget it.

"Warrior."

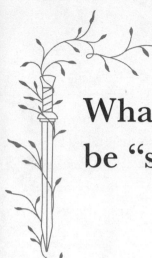

Chapter 1

What does it mean to be "suitable" anyway?

"Are you ready?" my dad whispered, squeezing my hand tucked under his arm. Dressed in white, I waited anxiously alongside him on the other side of the double-closed doors. The song that had accompanied the bridesmaids as they walked down the aisle stopped, and I heard the booming voice of our pastor.

"It is not good for man to be alone, so God created a helper suitable for him."

At that pronouncement, the doors swung open and there I stood. The *helper*. The bridal song played, and Dad and I marched toward my groom. While I had no idea what a helper was, I was absolutely in favor of a God who understood we were meant to be together.

I'll be honest with you: writing this project was a struggle. I knew what I wanted to say, I knew how I wanted it to sound, but it wasn't *flowing*. Ninety days before the manuscript was due, I was in a retreat setting with prayer teams made available for specific requests or just for listening. I approached two women and said rather directly, "I am working on a book about women, and I want it to pour out of me. I want to ask for an overflowing cup of creativity and clarity ..." I then promptly closed my eyes, put out my hands, and as efficiently as I could, prepared to "hurry up and receive." I felt like I had just invited Jesus to join one of the to-do lists that my colleague and I regularly share on a productivity app. Here's the task, and I want Him to help me do it with ease and excellence.

The women started to pray, and it was meaningful and sincere. They prayed over my mind, relationships, and research. I was encouraged and hopeful, and then, *bam*. The Holy Spirit matched my directness. *I am not your employer, your colleague, or your genie. I am your Father. You don't work for Me, you abide in Me. This isn't something to accomplish but rather a testimony to share. Let's have a conversation about creation and women, and you share with others where you've grown and been wrong and what you've learned.*

Right from the start, I want to be clear about what this is not. It is not a manifesto on how women are better than men. It's not an attempt to be controversial, or relevant. This work is the opposite of relevant, meaning recent; it's actually closer to ancient.

I am hoping to appeal not to your intellect, or your political persuasions, but to your intuition. Regardless of your gender, I have a feeling what I will share you've kind of always known, even if you didn't have words for it. During my experience these last couple of years working on this manuscript, when people asked what I was writing and I told them the thesis, they nodded with understanding. I didn't so much have to teach them anything as give words to, or reveal, what they already suspected. I hope it feels like I am handing you a shoe that fits perfectly and once you put it on, you'll never want to take it off.

This book records my questions and stories. It contains facts, insights I've learned from others, a bunch of experiences, and an honest grappling with this topic. I haven't wrestled with whether God's Word is truth, but with how this truth impacts my way of being. For decades I had been questioning *What is the role of a woman?* but God wants to *love* us far more than He wants to *use* us. This isn't a discussion about roles; it's a conversation about design. We marvel at His design in creation, how the solar system works, or the ecosystem, or the central nervous system ... He is perfect and does everything with purpose, so what is the purpose of uniquely making a man and a woman who correspond to each other? And my questions are just getting started. Can I correspond to my friends? Can I "help" my children? My coworkers? My brother? My pastor? Join me in asking good questions and engaging those around you in meaningful conversation. I pray this journey feels gentle, fierce, winsome, and serious.

Before modern-day Christianity, before the many lessons we'll learn about church history, before patriarchal societies and your premarital counseling, before X (Twitter) and #Metoo and feminism, there was Genesis and the creation account. We will start our conversation there because *He* starts the conversation there.

> The LORD God said, "It is not good for the man to be alone. I will make a helper suitable for him."
>
> Now the LORD God had formed out of the ground all the wild animals and all the birds in the sky. He brought them to the man to see what he would name them; and whatever the man called each living creature, that was its name. So the man gave names to all the livestock, the birds in the sky and all the wild animals.
>
> But for Adam no suitable helper was found. So the LORD God caused the man to fall into a deep sleep; and while he was sleeping, he took one of the man's ribs and then closed up the place with flesh. Then the LORD God made a woman from the rib he had taken out of the man, and he brought her to the man.
>
> The man said,
> "This is now bone of my bones
>   and flesh of my flesh;
> she shall be called 'woman,'
>   for she was taken out of man."

> That is why a man leaves his father and mother and is united
> to his wife, and they become one flesh.
>
> Adam and his wife were both naked, and they felt no shame.
> (Genesis 2:18–25)

Genesis 2:18 is the first time we see the word *ezer* used in the Bible. We'll end up reading it another twenty times in the Old Testament, but let's start here. "It's not good for man to be alone, so God made a helper (*ezer*) suitable (*kenegdo*) for him."

English Bibles translate *ezer* as "helper" and *kenegdo* as "suitable" or, in older translations, "meet," which helps us understand where we get *helpmeet* or, eventually, *helpmate*. *Kenegdo* is best understood as "an opposite," "counterpart," or "alongside." It implies that on their own, both men and women were lacking, but together they perfectly complemented each other. *Helpmate* today is seen as a pejorative term, and many modern women cringe at its use, but English doesn't do justice to the idea or picture of *ezer kenegdo*. *Ezer* ("helper") is a term of strength, and we'll read how God uses it to describe Himself when He comes to the rescue of His people.

The translation of the term *helpmate* led to interpretations of the woman's responsibility to assist the man in whatever he undertook—to "help" him on his mission in life—and over time, the belief that God gave the most important roles to men and supporting responsibilities to women. It facilitated a belief system that women were considered second-class citizens in the home and church, even when evidence, history, and calling showed otherwise.

The world—with few exceptions—practiced this idea of male dominance in the cultural construct of patriarchy (more on that next chapter). It meant for thousands of years, women had no rights to own property, speak on their own behalf, or have agency over their lives and choices. It doesn't make sense that the Church would adopt this so completely and not ask itself: Would our good God really condone a practice that considers something made in His own image as unworthy or weak or incomplete?

Kenegdo ("suitable") indicates the ezer is the man's match—literally "as in front of him, or corresponding to him." Theologian Victor Hamilton put it: "[*Kenegdo*] suggests that what God creates for Adam will correspond to him. Thus the new creation will be neither a superior nor an inferior, but an equal. The creation of this helper will form one-half of a polarity and will be to man as the South Pole is to the North Pole."[1] We are matched, corresponding, and need one another to paint a more complete picture of this mysterious and glorious creation.

Many times, Hebrew words paint a word picture, and when explaining this concept, rabbis talk about two planks. Picture them propped up against each other, forming a triangle. If one moves, the other plank falls over because the first plank is opposing it or holding it up. This is the picture of *suitable*. It's an intelligent design, with us each bearing a semblance of our Creator.

The first time my heart wrapped itself around this truth, I felt a profound sense of relief. Not because I was in a male-dominated marriage, or church, or social setting; it actually had nothing to do with the men in my life and how they had or hadn't treated me. (I have some great men around me.) I was relieved because I wanted to believe God liked us as much as it seemed He did men and we had an important, corresponding role to play in this earthly existence, that our plank was essential.

I was relieved because I wanted to believe God liked women as much as it seemed He did men.

God made us with purpose, and we are not from the leftover. Our very sense of being and calling comes from the word He uses to describe us: *ezer*. So, in my everyday working-mothering-friending-wifeing-living-and-loving life, what does that mean; what are the implications of being made a suitable helper?

If supporting one another was always God's plan, where did it go wrong?

Questions to Consider

Take a moment and pray about *suitable* and *helper*. As separate ideas, what do they mean to you? How about them together?

What did you grow up thinking was the role of women?

Who has influenced how you think about women?

When has God offered you help you couldn't give yourself?

Journal

What do you wish you had understood about *suitable* before now?

Chapter 2

What is there to fight about if Genesis 1 and 2 show us God's intended design?

"Call it the Human Mission—to be all and do all God sent us here to do. And notice—the mission to be fruitful and conquer and hold sway is given both to Adam and to Eve. 'And God said to them …' Eve is standing right there when God gives the world over to us. She has a vital role to play; she is a partner in this great adventure. All that human beings were intended to do here on earth—all the creativity and exploration, all the battle and rescue and nurture—we were intended to do together. In fact, not only is Eve needed, but she is desperately needed."[2]

Stasi Eldredge, *Captivating*

The Old Testament uses *ezer* in three distinct ways, twenty-one different times:

- To define woman (Genesis 2:18, 20).
- To describe allied soldiers who assist in battle (Joshua 1:14; 1 Chronicles 12:1–22) and for nations to whom Israel appealed for military aid (Isaiah 30:5; Ezekiel 12:14; Daniel 11:34).

- To describe God, as Israel's helper (Genesis 49:25; Exodus 18:4;
  Deuteronomy 33:7; 2 Chronicles 32:8; Psalms 10:14; 20:2;
  33:20; 70:5; 89:19; Isaiah 41:10–14).

Ezer is used consistently in a military context. It's the kind of help you need when the stakes are high and you're unable to help yourself; for example, when Israel sought military aid or help from her neighbors. God is His people's shield and defense, better than chariots and horses, and standing sentry watch over His people. The twenty other times the word is used, the person being described is God Himself, when you need Him to come through for you desperately. This is not an assistant role; the ezer *rescues*, is a lifesaver.

Hebrew scholar Robert Alter said the phrase *ezer kenegdo* is best translated as "sustainer beside him."[3] This translation hints at the idea we can't do it without the other. In Genesis 2, some have tried to make *ezer kenegdo* a "happy helper" or "teacher's aide," which has roots in patriarchy and chauvinism, not in Scripture. Consider this passage from Psalm 121, which we sing in popular modern-day worship songs.

> I lift my eyes up to the mountains,
> Where does my *ezer* come from?
> My *ezer* comes from YHWH
> The Maker of Heaven and Earth

No one thinks of God in that context as the "happy helper"! The writer of this psalm isn't asking where his aide is. He's asking where relief is coming from. Where is the strength he needs coming from? It's an important word that says a lot about how men and women should understand each other and the way we were created to interact together. We have all worked this out in our own ways since creation, relying (or not) on one another's strengths to accomplish goals or run a household, but today's conversation is about value, influence, authority, and power. How did God create men and women to come together, what was His idea, and who have I let teach me about this? And I kept asking myself during my initial study of ezer, *why haven't I asked these questions before?*

Whether I was willing to admit it or not, I had absorbed (at no fault of anyone) the subtle idea that men were *preferred*. Maybe not better, but certainly favored. The Bible has more stories of men than women, the coolest kingdom jobs seemed to go to them, they were outwardly stronger in many ways, they were created first ... I was beginning to ask, *why?* And more importantly, *does it matter?*

I asked myself if, at the end of this journey, I find out we are supposed to help men in their mission, or they are better/first, am I okay with it? We are called to follow Christ in His humility and meekness, not His power. If He asks me to lay my life down, go last, submit myself to others, spend my whole life in servant-hood, and be misunderstood, and underappreciated ... can I get comfortable with that?

He did.

This can't be a quest to be better, or else it's fundamentally not biblical. The Jesus way says we are to outdo one another in showing honor (Romans 12:10) and do nothing from rivalry or conceit but in humility count others more significant than ourselves (Philippians 2:3).

And that brings me to a fear I had about embarking on this work. In rightsizing this creation story in my mind, would I stoke in myself and any readers a sense of pride, rebellion, or bitterness? That isn't my goal; it's the exact opposite. I want to describe, discover, and call out women in their glory, with all the beauty they possess. When you see a woman who isn't striving to be anything other than exactly who she is, she's breathtaking. When a woman knows her worth, or that she is enough, she carries peace and gives it away liberally.

I am hoping to resolve for myself who God made woman to be. To stop the noise and power struggles and just *settle into it.* In the beginning of the Book, in the Garden, God intended women to act divine—sustaining, life-giving, and helping. Women were created to engage with His story and with His Adam. At the end of the Book, we as the Church are called the "bride of Christ." We will be together with God. I know there's always been a value and place held for our gender. We don't need to scream it, march about it, or demand it. It already *is*. Let's just discover what it means to be in this story and correspond biblically with our Adams and other Eves.

Genesis 1 and 2 paint a picture of the woman as ezer, who provides help man can't give himself, and then in chapter 3, gender hierarchy appears for the first time. "Your desire will be for your husband, and he will rule over you" (Genesis 3:16). But this distinction comes after the fall! The same fall that fractured both man and woman's relationship with God, and ultimately with each other. I don't want to emulate *that* model; that's the broken one. I want to take my cues on human relationships from the perfect design before sin entered the world. How He *intended* us to be. Ultimately, Eve will be held responsible for her sin before God, and if she was a second-class creation, then there will be a bigger reprimand for Adam, but we read they are equally held to account.

So, created equal, yet corresponding in that creation. Equally sinful, yet with unique consequences.

Is this where it all went wrong? Does all the pain and unfair treatment of women over all history originate in Genesis 3? Staying in Genesis, chapters 1 and 2 are two variants of the creation story. Chapter 1 is in a nice order and is what we usually teach from and record in children's books. God made light, sky, plants, space, sea creatures, land animals, and humans, male and female. Then He rested.

Chapter 2 has a different order and seems like almost a different story. God created man, *then* the Garden and plants, then animals, and finally, woman. In verse 2:18, God had not found a matching mate for Adam and said, "I will make a helper suitable for him." Then in the next verse, after God said it was not good for man to be alone, He made animals—He had not *already* made them. It's almost like God was searching for who would be a good enough helper for man. Read it below in the KJV version. God was looking to make something that would be a good helper, but none were ezer kenegdo.

> And the LORD God said, It is not good that the man should be alone; I will make him a help meet for him.

And out of the ground the LORD God formed every beast of the field, and every fowl of the air; and brought them unto Adam to see what he would call them: and whatsoever Adam called every living creature, that was the name thereof.

And Adam gave names to all cattle, and to the fowl of the air, and to every beast of the field; but for Adam there was not found a help meet for him.

And the LORD God caused a deep sleep to fall upon Adam, and he slept: and he took one of his ribs, and closed up the flesh instead thereof;

And the rib, which the LORD God had taken from man, made he a woman, and brought her unto the man.

And Adam said, This is now bone of my bones, and flesh of my flesh: she shall be called Woman, because she was taken out of Man.

Therefore shall a man leave his father and his mother, and shall cleave unto his wife: and they shall be one flesh.

And they were both naked, the man and his wife, and were not ashamed. (Genesis 2:18–25 KJV)

The *Midrash* is a recorded commentary where rabbis have debated the meaning of Scripture using other scriptures and historical documents. In it, they interpret Eve was not made from the head, where she would lord over man, nor from the foot, where she would be under man, but from the rib, where she would stand side by side, or equal, to man.

Everything else God tried to make wasn't suitable for man, so He put him to sleep to clone him. God built woman and brought her to the man. It was a powerful statement He was making: God stopped what He had been doing in creation to put man to sleep to *replicate* him. What does that say about how important women are? I am not sure, but it feels significant. And why hadn't I thought about this before? Why is all the debate in the creation story about old earth and new earth or was it a literal seven days? Why aren't we talking about the differences between chapters 1 and 2 and what that means for this gender discussion?

God stopped what He had been doing in creation to put man to sleep to *replicate* him. What does that say about how important women are?

In the first two chapters of Genesis, we are presented with a universe of how it's "supposed to be." Then after Adam and Eve ate the fruit of the Tree of Knowledge of Good and Evil and were cursed, what does it say? She would get pain in childbirth and her desire would now be for her husband and he would rule over her. So, did she also get the curse of patriarchy?[4] Of being dominated the rest of her existence? Are we fighting as Christians to uphold a *curse*? Think about the ways we try to mitigate the other consequences of the fall. I know people with pet snakes. We don't hesitate to give epidurals, so childbirth isn't painful anymore. For man's curse, the land was filled with thorns and thistles, and he would only eat from the sweat of his brow. Why are we using weed killers to remove thorns and thistles and have machines and technology of every kind to make work easier? We are mitigating the other consequences of the fall as much as possible, so why are we not trying to take this curse of patriarchy away? *Why this weird dominance and pressure on the neck of a gender who was made in the image of God?*

Some people are saying this, but maybe not often enough or not loud enough. I am hoping to add my voice to theirs, to stir conversations that drive us back to

Scripture and into a posture of spiritual curiosity. Consider this 2022 article in *Christianity Today*:

> It's a mistake to see Genesis 3 as a paradigm for human relationships and especially male-female ones. This text is describing the consequences of human rebellion, not God's original intention....
>
> God didn't desire thorns, thistles, and male domination any more than expectant parents carefully design a time-out corner for their children before they're born. If we want to recapture God's vision for creation, then, we need to lean in to Genesis 1 and 2 instead, where men and women stand side by side as allies in the work God designed for us to do.[5]

And authors like Baylor University professor Dr. Beth Allison Barr, who wrote this:

> It is in Genesis 3:16 (God speaking to the woman) where we first see hierarchy in human relationships.... Hierarchy was not God's will for the first pair, but it was imposed when they chose to disregard his command and eat the forbidden fruit.... Adam would now be subject to his source (the ground), even as Eve was now subject to her source (Adam). This was the moment of the birth of patriarchy. As a result of their sin, the man was now the master over the woman, and the ground was now master over the man, contrary to God's original intention in creation. Patriarchy wasn't what God wanted; patriarchy was a result of human sin.[6]

Are people talking like this in premarital counseling sessions? Is this thinking infiltrating the conversations going on about whether men and women can be friends? How does this inform our thinking about women in leadership?

What would it look like if instead of challenging men, or competing with men, we were on the lookout for when the Intelligent Designer called for us to correspond to and offer backing to men? Or ask for backing from them? Let's ask Him to teach us what He always intended. I just want to be and do and serve as He designed. I don't care where this journey ends; my life is not my own—I was bought with a price. I'll accept whatever He wants. I just want to know it for myself and not absorb a biased cocktail of church history and current cultural wars.

God is intentional, perfect, and sovereign. What *was* His plan in making us? The answer, I am hoping, has more to do with who I am than what I can do. This can't just be a conversation about authority, position, rights ... it's more primal than that. It must unlock identity. That's what I am hungry to be fed: biblical truth, ancient biblical truth, on His original purpose for ezer.

Questions to Consider

Look up the other uses of *ezer* in the Bible. What does that add to this discussion?

Did you also grow up wondering if God preferred men?

How do the varying creation accounts impact this conversation?

Journal

This topic raises all kinds of questions in me. What questions does it stir in you?

Chapter 3

Why isn't the Church leading this conversation instead of lagging?

As I shared with people what I was writing, I frequently heard, "Really? What makes you want to get into all of that?" As if there was already some fatigue and weariness around the subject. Maybe there is for some, but it's concerning to me that this next generation of women is growing up and not finding a place in the church or the kingdom to use their gifts. They are leaders, but not always allowed in the decision-making rooms. They are pastors, but typically to share only with other women or children. They are creative, discerning, wise, and strong, but often kept behind the scenes. The Church should be leading this conversation, as Jesus did in His time, but instead we lag.

A consequence of the church's posture drives women to use their gifts in secular workspaces where they can advance in secular boardrooms. While it's important to be salt and light, and there's tremendous value in workplace ministry, we need women's voices everywhere. I long for the young women in my life to see every field as wide open. If they are strategic thinkers, powerful communicators, creatives, financially driven, and natural leaders, I want them to believe they can listen for God to call them to serve—inside or outside the church.

At the heart of a woman is a longing to *co-* (co-create, co-llaborate, co-mission ...), to share life together; it's part of her relational God-stamped nature. Regardless of vocation or personality, she has a primary role, even if her title is assistant and her giftings take her into the background. Her story is critical and her *yes* needed. Every ezer has a calling, an irreplaceable role; the Bible calls it "good works ordained in advance for her to do" (Ephesians 2:10). She was created with tenacity, loyalty, a willingness to sacrifice, and dreams. We have to do more than just make room for her; we must believe in her inherent value.

We have to do more than just make room for her; we must believe in her inherent value.

Dr. Dean Nicholas is a friend and scholar in Hebrew language studies. As I was wrestling with this passage, I visited him.

"So, I want to ask you about the Hebrew word *ezer*." He smiled, and I felt heartened by his encouragement. "Just read to me Genesis 2 in Hebrew, translating as you go, and tell me what it means. I am hearing it means 'warrior,' and I am hearing it *can't* mean 'warrior,' and honestly, I am confused."

He opened his Bible and started reading. I closed my eyes and listened to the poetic nature of this passage and the familiar account of creation. As he got closer to verse 18, I held my breath.

"It was not good for man to be alone, so God created a corresponding help—"

I couldn't stop myself. I interrupted before he could continue. "So, does 'warrior' work? What does 'help' even mean here? Which one is it?"

"Yes," he said, which didn't exactly answer my question. "Yes, it means 'help,' and yes, it has a military connotation. It's the kind of help you need and can't provide yourself."

I must have looked confused, because he took out a sticky note and drew four circles, connecting the one representing God with the one representing man and woman and all of them over nature. "This was the original plan, how the Garden and creation were designed. It was what it was supposed to be. God in perfect harmony with man, man in perfect harmony with woman, and they were in perfect harmony with nature. This is the way God made things to be; this is the *shalom* of God's creation." I sighed; that seemed a long time ago.

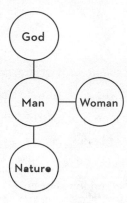

He continued, "Then the fall happened, and when these bonds broke, there was no longer *shalom* between any of it. All connection was broken. God no longer walked daily with the humans in the Garden. The relationship changed between the man and the woman. He was now over her, nature worked against them—snakes bit, childbirth was painful, weeds made farming harder—and in the end, we were cursed to return to the dirt from which we were made. This was the fall and the curse it brought. And the following chapters show that these curses continued. Brother killed brother, the world filled with violence, and the Tower of Babel scattered people who couldn't understand each other anymore. God was upset that He had even made people and decided to kill them all except for Noah and his family. So, He flooded the world and destroyed almost everything! The bonds between humans and God and humans and nature were broken in the fall. And we still feel the effects of this fall!" He got another Post-it note and drew the same four circles, but now without any connection between them.

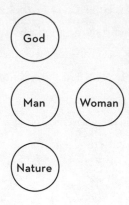

Seeing the discouraged look on my face, he pressed on. "Then Jesus came into the picture. He declared that the great restoration the prophets had foretold, the restoring of the bonds, had begun (Luke 4:16–20). And think about His ministry on earth in the context of the bonds: He was in perfect communion with God the Father, whom He called *Abba*; He cared for the outsiders and marginalized people and tells us to pray for and love our enemies, turn the other cheek, go the extra mile. And think about all His miracles—healed the sick, restored sight to the blind, raised the dead, calmed the sea, walked on water. This was not Jesus saying, 'Look—I have power and can do stuff you cannot!' These were evidence of the kingdom of God at hand! The bonds were restored. That is why when Jesus sent out the disciples, they were shocked that they could perform miracles too."

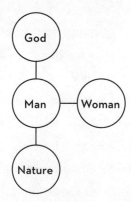

With finality, he pulled off the last Post-it note and drew dotted lines between the four circles. "But this is where we are now, in what theologians call the Church Age. We are living in a time of 'now, but not yet,' where we see glimpses of God's kingdom now, but still experience the brokenness in the world, created by the fall. So, it's now our job as Jesus' followers to demonstrate to people what God's kingdom looks like, giving glimpses of His *shalom*. It is our responsibility to show others what was intended, to live and relate to God, each other, and nature in the way God created it. Because it's not just what was long ago; it is what will one day be again. Now in part, one day in full!"

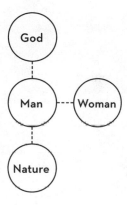

How *did* He create us? How can I reflect that in my life and relationships? I looked at the circles and the dotted lines and thought about the tremendous responsibility to look like Jesus. I felt reminded again this isn't a political issue, a gender issue, or a culture war. This ezer business involves trying to understand how He *made* us as women and how we live as we were designed, here in the "now but not yet …"

"So, can I write about *ezer* as 'warrior'?" I asked, getting back to my original question.

"Yes," he said, "she can be used by God to make the impossible possible with her efforts. Looking at the other texts with this word, it's safe to say she was designed to be fully engaged, offering rescue/help, as God Himself did to Israel."

We've never been in a more confusing time regarding gender and gender roles. There are debates and church splits, broken marriages, hurting children, op-eds and college courses, new terms, and social media. We are not in a restored creation; we live in an Order of Brokenness. It's this "now, but not yet ..." One day this question will be null; we will all be living fully within the design God intended. But today we are stuck in this cracked world, with fragmented understanding and wrecked systems. Since it's our job to reflect as much as possible the kingdom of heaven on earth, we have this conversation to help fix what's broken and to better reflect creation as it was intended.

How do we accomplish this goal?

By being curious students and asking God for discernment.

We are relational because the triune God, three-in-one, is relational and we are made in His image. As a result, we are filled with a desire to be known. The Bible is principally a love story between God and His people. We can know others because He first knows us. And now, we can express that supernatural love by co-creating, offering, and bonding—the rich activities of connection.

Jesus came down to show us a kingdom way of life, a connected, Eden-like heaven on earth. He was the fulfillment of prophecy, and His birth began to teach us how differently He was going to operate in a world already set up with systems and practices. Jesus could have been born in any manner, at any time, and anywhere. His choices put on display His *way*, and He's been asking us to model that *way* ever since.

Jesus' very birth contrasted two kingdoms. There already was a king of the Jews, Herod, backed by the power of the Roman Empire. An incredible engineer and fabulously wealthy, he built a mountain with a palace on top in case anyone wondered where the king lived. The other king, this new king, baby Jesus, was born to a poor, rejected family from rural Nazareth ("can anything good come out of Nazareth?" John 1:46) just a few miles away, literally in the shadow of this mountain.

From the beginning, Jesus made a point—an introduction to this upside-down way of thinking. Shepherds, the marginalized of society, announced His arrival. This kingdom wasn't supposed to "make sense," it was from another place. This baby would grow up, and in His teaching ministry, Jesus would say those who belong in the kingdom of heaven are poor in spirit, meek, pure in heart, peacemakers ... "for they will be called children of God" (Matthew 5:9). Because He made us, He knows it's best for us to act this way. We all have dozens of cautionary tales of people who weren't poor in spirit, meek, pure in heart, or peacemakers and how their stories ended. Wherever this biblical journey takes us, we can agree, God's way is best, even if it's unfamiliar.

Jesus tells us to turn the other cheek and, when someone wants our shirt, to give him our tunic—the first shall be last, and the last shall be first; these ideas are a reversal of society—and to embrace this new kingdom theology. His followers had to change everything about how they saw the world, including the treatment of women. We'll read lots of passages where Jesus treated women with respect and dignity because the Bible says He only did what He saw His Father doing. The Creator of ezer knows what she is capable of. He made her that way, and so with confidence, Jesus gave women responsibilities, trusted their insight, and included them in His mission.

God fashioned His daughters to be ezer-warriors alongside our brothers, whether single or married, regardless of age, for the new in faith and the old saints. He knows where He is calling the ezer. He sends her to break man's loneliness by passionately walking and fighting alongside him. Man needs everything she brings to their mission. When women's voices are excluded from conversations, only a partial perspective is offered, and we bench half the army. We are better when we come together, because this is how God designed it. It's ancient and primal, and our intuition knows it's true. And ezers need men too. We'll talk about what that looks like and how even when it's messy it's still good.

We can learn from God how to best offer help, how to ezer with strength, and how to be alert to the needs of others. It isn't a luxury to think about these things; we can falsely believe only *some* women deserve to live alive or strong. Or only *some* can be loved or have an adventure or correspond with another. But nothing could be further from the truth; this isn't the right of extra-godly women, older women, beautiful women, special women ... ezer doesn't have to try harder, be better. She can just *be*, as she was created.

Questions to Consider

What do you see as evidence that we live in the "now, but not yet"?

What has been your experience as a woman within the Church?

What role does discernment play in this discussion?

Journal

Has your experience as a woman been more of a Genesis 2 (co-creating and co-missioning alongside men) or a Genesis 3 experience (one gender ruling over another)?

Chapter 4

What does this mean if you *are* a woman, *live* with a woman, *love* a woman, *work* with a woman, are *raising* a woman, or have *been borne* from a woman?

(It means this conversation involves you.)

At a women's conference I recently attended, the day opened with an interesting exercise. During registration, the organizers gave each woman a bracelet that lit up. Later, the lights were extinguished and they asked everyone to turn on their bracelets. A dark auditorium was lit by a thousand small circles. Gradually, a screen instructed us to raise our hand if we read a sentence we identified with. The questions started easy:

"I am single." About a third of the hands shot in the air. You could see women looking around and feeling camaraderie with their fellow sisters.

"Someone invited me here." A hundred or so hands slid up. You no longer wondered if *everyone else* here knew each other.

"I am a mother, and I am missing out on a sports event today." More hands came up, and a small laugh rippled through the room.

Slowly, hands went up and down as identifiers continued to flash on the screen, helping create the feeling *your people* were there.

Then the mood in the room became more vulnerable ...

"I feel alone often." *Hands raised.*

"I struggle with body image." *Most of the room responded.*

"I am proud of something I've recently accomplished."

"I am grieving someone."

As the music played softly in the background, and hands slipped up and down, we saw that while our circumstances are unique, women can be diverse and yet similar. We are not just one category; we carry many qualities simultaneously. The same exercise would be equally effective at a men's gathering, but I was struck by how we can put women in a singular category depending on whether she works or not, whether she's married or not, or whether she has birthed children or not.

The more closely women can embody who we are, the better we can represent ourselves to others. Women are more than our status; we are thoughtful, healing, and creative, and we can hold dozens of other characteristics simultaneously. My mother used to tell me, "We teach people how to treat us." For me, that has looked like if I am in a situation where women are devalued, I might have to work harder to "introduce" myself and not allow disrespect. Can I be winsome about it? Yes. I don't have to be aggressive. But the way we, and other women, allow ourselves to be treated isn't solely the responsibility of the men in our lives.

One of the churches where I regularly communicate has been wrestling with whether women can sit on the elder board, and it was creating a lot of pain and division in the body. There were gatherings, social media posts, and finally an open congregational meeting. I sat quietly in the back, listening to both sides, brothers and sisters who were honestly seeking the Lord and longing to be biblically based. I texted my husband, Todd, who couldn't be there, "Earnest. Everyone looks so keen on doing God's will. It feels like we should have consensus with all this goodwill going around."

Finally, someone called on me, "Beth, what do *you* think?"

I knew what I said would be simultaneously applauded by some, misunderstood by others, and later quoted. Could I say something that would unite the body?

"So far, this has been a conversation about authority, and that's not something man can give or take away. My spiritual authority comes from being a co-heir with Christ. What we are longing for as women is *influence*. The chance to shape this community and speak in its direction. If I had to choose between influence and authority, I'd pick influence every time. And I believe the women in this room affect the men in this room. No rules or policies can change that; it's inevitable."

If I had to choose between influence and authority, I'd pick influence every time.

The larger conversation we're having has two distinct levels. On one level, *how do ezers wake up and fulfill their calling within the context of their relationships and the stories they are called into?* On another level, *how does the body of Christ organize itself in a way that most closely reflects God's original purpose?* As a woman, the latter is my main focus since that's all I have control over. However, let's take a moment to address the Church before we settle into where most of our time will be spent: *how do I understand and live as an ezer?*

The Church falls all over the place on this discussion. Some denominations do not allow women to hold the office of pastor, and in others, women can hold any office. Once when I was speaking at a university chapel, I had a curious experience. While we were doing sound checks, I noticed staff members pulling the podium down from the stage to sit on the floor. "Oh, I am glad to be down here," I exclaimed. "I like being able to see faces and interact in a way I can't from the stage."

"That works out great," said the service coordinator, "because we don't allow women to speak from the stage."

I didn't want to seem contentious, but I wondered if their theology was truly based on the six-feet height difference of a platform. Who created that rule, and how did it make them feel safer to have me on the floor? I have dozens of these stories: churches changing their minds at the last minute, or a pastor asking me a few questions onstage so that when I preached it would be considered an "interview." God bless the Church; while trying to hold tightly to Scripture, she has created all kinds of work-arounds. This is not the topic of this book—whether women should be pastors—but it's an example of the larger dysfunction that's now out in the open.

The truth is, I have an audience of One, and He hears me whether I am on the floor or the stage, whether I speak to thousands or just my windshield. I am called to worship, and who and how it's received isn't mine to control. But still … Church, let's keep inviting women to the table, into the room, onto the stage, *if that's her gift*. If she wants other behind-the-scenes roles because that's how she's made and where she's called, hallelujah! Let's just give her the same choices as her brother.

In a 2023 interview on the *Russell Moore* podcast, *Purpose Driven Life* author Rick Warren detailed how his thinking had changed on women in pastoral leadership. As a result of his work with the movement Finishing the Task, he studied afresh the Great Commission found in Matthew 28: "Then Jesus came to them and said, 'All authority in heaven and on earth has been given to me. Therefore go and make disciples of all nations, baptizing them in the name of the Father and of the Son and of the Holy Spirit, and teaching them to obey everything I have commanded you. And surely I am with you always, to the very end of the age'" (verses 18–20).

Of the four actions to obey in that command (go, make disciples, baptize, and teach), he noted that God doesn't ask or give that authority only to men. This command was for both genders, and we see Jesus' disciples believed it, because about a month later when they gathered for the day of Pentecost, everyone played a part, speaking and "declaring the wonders of God" (Acts 2:11). We know it was both men and women because Peter felt the need to explain what they were seeing.

> Then Peter stood up with the Eleven, raised his voice and addressed the crowd: "Fellow Jews and all of you who live in Jerusalem, let me explain this to you; listen carefully to what I say. These people are not drunk, as you suppose. It's only nine in the morning! No, this is what was spoken by the prophet Joel:
>
> "'In the last days, God says,
>   I will pour out my Spirit on all people.
> *Your sons and daughters* will prophesy,
>   your young men will see visions,
>   your old men will dream dreams.
> Even on my servants, both men and women,
>   I will pour out my Spirit in those days,
>   and they will prophesy.'" (Acts 2:14–18)

The church grew in the first three hundred years in a way it hasn't since. I wonder why. Could it be we injected our culture and politics into the gospel and took one apostle's words, Paul's (more on this in a bit), spoken within a particular culture and often misunderstood, and raised them above the actions and teachings of Jesus? Could the slowdown in the growth of the Church be in part a result of benching half the team (quieting women, allowing them to only use their gifts in certain settings, and excluding them from discussions, decisions, and leadership rooms)?

Does it even make sense that God would create us both in His image, give us authority to go, make disciples, baptize, and teach, and then muzzle 50 percent of us?

My great-grandmother was a pastor, and I am sure one reason I am unafraid to fill a pulpit is because someone taught someone, who taught someone, who taught me ... women can divide the Scripture with authority. I am grateful for those "some-ones" in my life, but all too aware that for others, someone taught someone taught someone differently. How do we sort through our backgrounds, our influences, and the world's messages to land on good theology? Women in the church today reckon with some serious lies:

- We are the sum total of our appearance.
- Spiritual women are busy and dutiful.
- God is just like my earthly father.
- I can't help how I am.
- I am only complete if I am coupled with a man.

This is just a sampling. We encounter lies about who we are and lies about how we are to act around men.

More than God wanting us to think in right ways, He longs for us to reflect Him. We will become more like Him, not by being more disciplined, but by falling in love with Him. God wants us to want Him, to "seek Him with all our hearts" (see Jeremiah 29:13) as He wants us. Tozer said, "God waits to be wanted." That longing and wanting we experience with God impact the longing and wanting we experience with men. There is just so *much* (chemistry, history, connection) between men and women, over time the Church developed two distinct camps in an attempt to organize ourselves.

There are two theological views on the relationship between men and women, especially relating to marriage and ministry. One is called "complementarianism" and the other is "egalitarianism." Interestingly, a generational break seems to have occurred in the understanding of these terms. When I ask younger women, they often don't know these two terms, what they mean, or their history. In case that's you, complementarianism stresses that although men and women are equal in personhood, they are created for different roles. Egalitarianism agrees that men and women are equal in personhood but holds there are no gender-based limitations on the roles of men and women.

Neither of these terms are in the Bible, but both camps have biblical reasons for their beliefs. Complementarians hold that masculinity and femininity were created by God as meaningful distinctions indicating different roles that, when embraced, will lead to the best possible spiritual well-being for believers. They believe men hold leadership positions and women should not be placed in authority over them. Ephesians 5 and 1 Timothy 2 are key passages for complementarians.

Egalitarians believe that men and women are equal in role capabilities and see no gender restrictions on what roles men and women can fulfill in the church, home, and society. Egalitarians hold to teachings that Jesus eliminated gender-specific, class, and race roles. They often quote Galatians 3:28, which says, "There is neither Jew nor Gentile, neither slave nor free, nor is there male and female, for you are all one in Christ Jesus."

Whichever resonates for you, we all must decide if it's something we hold on to "thickly" or "thinly." I want to resolve my conviction and belief on this and *then* decide which camp I belong to, not the other way around. Will this issue determine which church I attend? Which spouse I choose? How I raise my children? Too often we identify with a group of people and swallow their belief system without examination. What do you think the Bible teaches? Take a moment and allow yourself the reflection of who taught you about women. What did they teach you? If this is the first time you are thinking about these things, do you have good sounding boards around you? If you are married and you and your partner don't agree, what are your options?

Todd and I have sought to stay in the conversation together, trying out our thoughts and convictions in non-contentious settings and challenging each other to keep learning. It's made our journey gentle, and we determined wherever our orthodoxy (belief) landed us, our orthopraxy (conduct) would remain the same.

God's way is community, reliance on each other, and submission to one another. He taught us to be at peace with one another and to wash each other's feet. Through Paul, God said, be devoted to one another and honor one another above ourselves. Live in harmony and stop passing judgment. Instruct one another, accept one another, wait for one another, serve one another, carry the other's burden, be patient, kind, compassionate, forgiving, encouraging, and hospitable. However we determine to split the pot of power and authority in our marriage, this is how people will know we are His kids.

Men and women should unpack God's Word together on this. If only women learn about women, it's not going to work out well for the Church. Both genders need to understand the implications of this message. So, if you *are* a woman, *live* with a woman, *love* a woman, *work* with a woman, are *raising* a woman, or have *been borne* from a woman, this conversation involves you.

I asked some ezer-related questions on my social media platforms, and I'll include some of those insights going forward, mainly because hearing others process this and ask questions encourages me. One woman posted vulnerably:

> Being a warrior sounds like there's a place for me at the table and in the fight. I get to take up space. I'm meant to take up space, to have a voice and a role. A helper feels more like trying to squeeze in where there's room. To not take up too much space or be too loud or have an agenda. A warrior feels like a team. A helper feels like being shrunk to fit into an easily digestible package.

May we stay in the conversation until our families and churches understand we all benefit from the space women occupy.

Questions to Consider

Have you ever had to teach someone how to treat you?

What is the difference to you between authority and influence?

Do you identify with complementarianism or egalitarianism? Why?

Journal

Take a moment to consider what lies about women you struggle with believing.

Chapter 5

Do you see this woman?

"A helper can bring her husband the screwdriver.
The warrior knows how to use it."

Cara Brueggeman Haas

Two weeks before Easter in 2020, the pastor at a large church in my city departed. With everyone going online for the pandemic, the church needed someone whom people recognized to serve as interim pastor. They asked if I was willing since I had guest-spoken there many times over the last decade. *But be a pastor?* What did I know about that?

Todd and I went for a walk and, in the privacy of our relationship, asked each other all the hard questions: *Did we think I had this calling? Did we think it was okay if I said yes? Can women be senior pastors? Did God give temporary assignments? Without formal training, could I hold a position of such spiritual authority? What did the Bible say? What would others say?* In every direction, we discussed it.

A principle that guides my decisions is a Hebrew word I learned years ago: *hineni*. It translates in our Bibles as "here I am," but a better translation is "whatever it is you are asking of me, I am already in agreement of it." I knew that (or I believed) God was asking this of me, so the answers to all my questions and insecurities would end with "yes." The majority of the church community embraced me in that role. It wasn't easy to lead a congregation used to a man, but ultimately, I found my gender benefited me. Instead of trying to be masculine—or worse yet, gender neutral—I determined I would use my femininity as a strength.

As an ezer leader, I am maternal; it's how He made me: a life-giver. Women bring forth, we incubate. We carry into the world new life, but we also breathe life into broken hearts and new dreams. Every time we cheer on, pick up, or prop up, we are acting like Jesus. So, yes to your idea, colleague, yes to trying again, and yes to the hard-is-worth-it. Let me encourage and breathe life into you ...

Feminine strength has been brutalized by an enemy whose sole function is to destroy God's creation, and Eve is the crown of creation. As suitable helpers, ezers embody beauty and the mystery of God in a way that compares to nothing else in all creation. If the enemy can destroy ezer or keep her captive, or deceive her with lies, he can ruin or derail her. I wrote a whole book about spiritual warfare and the posture of spiritual aggression. Against this enemy, we don't just put on our armor of God (Ephesians 6) and wait for him to come get us (1 Peter 5:8). He does nothing new to me or my gender; his tune hasn't changed since Genesis 2. I can see him a mile off, and I am not waiting for him to come get me. I will attack him first, using the tools of worship, prayer, Scripture, rest, fellowship, and fasting.

Jesus only ever did what the Bible says He saw His Father doing. He treated women with respect and dignity because that's how His Father taught Him. He gave them responsibilities, trusted their insight, and wove them into His ministry. The characteristics typically assigned to women—shielding, comforting, birthing, protecting, hovering—are God qualities and they manifest in us because we are of Him. We don't need to apologize for having those attributes or let someone mock us for exercising how God designed us.

Whether leading our families, our churches, or at our workplaces, we are called to be all we were made to be and let the questions of others fall around us, even the unanswered ones in our own minds. There's work to do, teams to lead, people to love, prompts to follow, projects to create, teachings to obey ... I remind myself liberally and surround myself with others who do the same: God is proud of how you model Him.

At its heart, this is an "and" conversation, not an "or." I have shied away from gender conversations because they tend to be "or" (women *or* men). Along with taking my cues from the Eden context, I want to study Jesus, who was radical in His approach toward women.

In John 4:4–42, when Jesus talked to the woman at the well—arguably the first missionary—He ignored two codes of behavior. He initiated a conversation with a foreigner, a Samaritan who was also a woman. "How can you, a Jew, ask me, a Samaritan woman, for a drink?" (verse 9 NABRE). Jesus recognized and honored her. When His disciples returned, they were uneasy with Jesus' behavior.

"What are you looking for? Why are you talking with her?" (verse 27 NABRE).

John made sure we knew that although a woman's testimony was not trustworthy, here the Samaritan woman's words were acted upon. "Many of the Samaritans of that town began to believe in him because of the word of the woman who testified, 'He told me everything I have done'" (verse 39 NABRE).

When I was a freshman in high school, my parents heard about a national ministry that was looking to plant chapters in local public high schools. They invited the organization's leader to our home so they could learn more about this opportunity. At one point, our guest excused me from our table and said he wanted to talk to my parents alone. I did what any fifteen-year-old girl would do: I went around the wall and listened from the other side.

"I think you have all the ingredients here to start a great club," he began. "But here's where I see a problem. We don't start with freshman girls; they don't hold the clout in the school ecosystem to get it started on the right foot. Do you know any other families that have older students whom we could invite into this conversation?" God *bless* him. Looking back, I understand where he was coming from. He had a winning formula and didn't want to deviate from it. But my dad wouldn't hear of it.

"Just wait a minute," he said, his voice raising. "Don't *ever* underestimate my freshman daughter."

That story in my life is more than three decades old, and my dad has long since passed, but I can still tell you what I was wearing and where I was standing when I heard those words. They landed in a tender place, where I've guarded them ever since. Proverbs 25:11 says, "Like apples of gold in settings of silver is a word aptly spoken" (TLV). When someone affirms you with spiritual authority, it moves you.

Jesus recognized the dignity of women in situations that, by ritual law, demanded judgment, like the sinful woman who anointed Jesus (Luke 7:36–50) or the woman caught in adultery (John 8:3–11) whom He saw as deserving compassion. After Jesus was touched and anointed by a woman who was a recognized sinner, we hear the expected reaction from Simon, his host. This prominent religious leader, a Pharisee, said, "If this man were a prophet, he would have known who and what sort of woman this is who is touching him, for she is a sinner" (Luke 7:39 ESV). Jesus told the woman her sins were forgiven but then also used her actions (and the love that prompted them) to teach His offended host. Jesus' question to him was pointed:

"Do you see this woman?" (Luke 7:44).

We can only guess why Simon was afraid. Why *are* some people afraid of women? What is it about our mystery? Our beauty? Our Eve-reputation of having wily ways? I am not sure what was happening with Simon, but it's often fear that leads to judgment. Jesus rose above all that and regularly conversed with women.

Martha and Mary are two examples we find in Luke 10:38–42. Mary is described as one who "sat beside the Lord at his feet listening to him speak" (verse 39 NABRE). To sit at the feet of a rabbi meant the person was his student. When men and women minister together, it's as the kingdom was designed. The default button of the earth is one to rule or control the other. In Matthew 12, Jesus stretched out His hand toward His disciples and said, "Here are my mother and my brothers" (verses 46–50). His use of *both* masculine and feminine words indicates some of His disciples were women.

Or consider that He first revealed Himself as resurrected to women. It's not that He revealed Himself to women *over* men or women *instead of* men. It's that He included women in the most important moment in history: *He is risen.* Following Jesus' example, we can be inclusive, without being divisive. We can be biblically

DO YOU SEE THIS WOMAN?

sound, and not political. Jesus revealed Himself first to women, and we know He did *nothing* by accident. So, what does that detail mean?

Following Jesus' example, we can be inclusive, without being divisive. We can be biblically sound, and not political.

Combining the accounts of all four gospels, we see several women present: Mary of Magdalene and the other Mary (Matthew 28:1), and Salome (Mark 16:1); Luke includes Joanna (Luke 24:10); Mark says that there were "many other women who had come up with him to Jerusalem" (Mark 15:41). And Luke agrees that other women were present (Luke 24:10). Mary Magdalene was a woman with a past; she had an ill repute, and yet ... God picked her.

She got the best assignment in the Bible: "Go tell My disciples I resurrected from the dead!" (see John 20:17).

Why didn't Jesus just go Himself to the disciples? What possibly were the reasons He chose to reveal Himself first to women?

It could be the women stayed with Him through the crucifixion, so He appeared first to those who had stuck with Him to the last. Or maybe since women traditionally carried out the burial rituals in first-century Judaism, they were witnesses by *default*. It could have been an apologetic choice: secular scholars say if you were going to make this up, women wouldn't be the first witnesses if you wanted first-century audiences to believe it. And it's unanimous—all the accounts are the same: women were the first to see Him resurrected. Or finally, it could have been Jesus was continuing His practice of elevating the status of women in general.

If He revealed Himself to women because women stuck with Him through the crucifixion, that makes sense to me. Women have a stick-to-it-ness about them, especially when it comes to someone they love. I've watched women stick by men who have failed them, children who are sick or wayward, and friends who need more than they give. In the fabric of our gender, we *stay*. I have a friend who adopted a set of older siblings and they have given her incredible grief over the years. One time I was in her living room and heard her daughter call her a swear word. My head swiveled to see her reaction, all the while wondering what *I* would do if someone said that to me. She didn't miss a beat—just maintained eye contact and said, "Yeah ... but I'm *your* bitch."

Looking past her use of profanity, she was demonstrating the pursuit of the gospel ... Jesus stuck with us and we can now stick with others. When I am tempted to forget and give up (on a circumstance, dream, healing, or relationship), I remember Isaiah 51:1: "Listen to me, you who pursue righteousness and who seek the LORD: Look to the rock from which you were cut and to the quarry from which you were hewn." This is what my family of God does: we stick together.

Jesus may have revealed Himself to women because women carried out burial rituals. In almost every corner of this world and throughout recorded history, women have been entrusted with the care of bodies. We birth them. We feed them. We wash, mend, comfort, and fret over them. It is unremarkable that women arrived at the tomb of Jesus to anoint Him for burial. The women who looked after Him in life came to care for His body one last time.

Further, if He revealed Himself to women first because they are elevated in God's kingdom, that's what He had been doing for the last three years. Jesus spoke to women in public. He cured a woman who had been crippled for eighteen years, laying hands on her in the temple and saying, "Woman, you are set free of your infirmity" (Luke 13:12). In another example, a leader of the synagogue became indignant that Jesus had healed a woman on the Sabbath. Jesus used a title of dignity for her, "daughter of Abraham" (Luke 13:16). (The expression "son of Abraham" was used to indicate a male Jew bound by covenant to God, but until then women had never been called "daughters of Abraham.") He just didn't worry about the societal rules; He did, said, acted, served, elevated, and talked to whomever, however, whenever He wanted, following the will of His Father.

One Sunday, when I was living as a missionary in Mexico, my pastor asked if anyone was willing to translate his message from Spanish to English for some visitors. I pretended I knew more Spanish than I did and eagerly raised my hand. Later, between the not-so-great acoustics, the speed at which he was passionately presenting, and the words we sometimes use in church but not in regular life, I got lost. I didn't want to *acknowledge* I was lost, but I knew we were in Ephesians, and I knew what I thought about Ephesians. So, when he took a breath, I filled it in with my thoughts on the passage, but not exactly a direct reflection of what he was saying.

After a couple more similar experiences, my pastor suggested we trade: I write the message and he translate for me. He had no model in his life for a female preacher, but he saw what God was doing and leaned in to it. He walked with me on that journey and is an example of a man who trusted an ezer.

God doesn't count like we do or see people like we do. He doesn't look at accomplishments or titles and prefer someone as a result. He saw who others didn't and spoke to them about their inherent value. When you have someone's full attention, you feel honored. We look like Him when we *honor* both men and women, the seemingly important people and the marginalized, those we agree with and those we think are crazy. Both men and women have a chance to follow His example, creating spaces for women. (We'll address in a later chapter how women can sometimes be competitive and how the culture of scarcity can cause some to feel there isn't enough for generosity.)

The final possibility for why Jesus revealed Himself first to women is that no one would have made it up that way. According to Josephus, the Jewish historian, and the Talmud, in the first century the testimony of women was not counted as credible and was considered unreliable at best. "But let not the testimony of women be admitted, on account of the levity and boldness of their sex ... since it is probable that they may not speak truth, either out of hope of gain, or fear of punishment."[7]

From Templeton Prize winner, Anglican priest, and physicist John Polkinghorne:

> Perhaps the strongest reason of taking the stories of the empty tomb absolutely seriously lies in the fact that it is women who play the leading role. It would have been very unlikely for anyone in the ancient world who was concocting a story to assign the principal part to women since, in those times, they were not considered capable of being reliable witnesses in a court of law. It is surely much more probable that they appear in the gospel accounts precisely because they fulfilled the role that the stories assigned to them, and in so doing, they make a startling discovery.[8]

Why didn't Jesus just fulfill this role Himself? *He* could have gathered the disciples. Instead, Jesus assigned the commission to Mary. It was intentional; He was making sure we understand we *all* qualify to tell of His resurrection. This is what Jesus left us to do. The relentlessness of an ezer-confident, unshakable security she is God's and God is hers spurs her on to offer help when the storms or circumstances are merciless. She can keep going ... This kind of faith or *chutzpah* led to the widow knocking insistently on the door, and the perfume bottle getting broken—regardless of who is watching.

Questions to Consider

What does it mean to contend for others?

How do we keep this as an "and" and not an "or" conversation?

How did Jesus recognize the dignity of women?

Journal

What rules of engagement do you think Jesus would ignore today?

Chapter 6

How did the early church treat women *after* Jesus turned everything upside down?

In writing this manuscript, I was reading commentaries, researching church history, and wrestling with the nuance of the subject when I traveled to Back2Back's India site. We had just opened a school, and I observed the new principal with her herculean task looking graceful and confident. I didn't need to understand the Hebrew distinction; I was looking at an ezer. With her education and experience, she was helping teachers, parents, and students form a working school with excellent results. When I asked why she was willing to work so hard when there were easier paths available, she shared God had prepared her by giving her a vision.

Later that week, we traveled to another partner school in a working slum. The director is a woman who took over the work first started by her mother. She shared the power of education to unlock an otherwise unavailable future. She also sees education as an excuse to connect with the community, using every existing training and tool at her disposal to strengthen families, preventing their rupture and further vulnerability. Again, here is a woman not spending one minute worried about what she is allowed to be or do biblically. She is looking at her Father and going *in*.

Finally, as God continued to make His point utterly clear to me, that same week we met with Tabitha, a woman who leads a Christian school within a

Muslim slum. She has been at this work for forty-five years, most of them as a widow. They held a school assembly for us, and both Hindu and Muslim mothers came to cheer on their children. There in the middle was Tabitha, looking regal and at ease with her calling and leadership, providing gospel clarity and a bright light within a dark context. We met with her in her office afterward, and I asked a few questions about her needs and prayer requests. Her responses demonstrated it wasn't her "job" that defined her as an ezer, but rather her faithful, long-term response to a call.

Contrast those stories with a recent conversation I had with a young staff woman, who was leaving the ministry because, after hearing a podcast about following your passion, she realized she wasn't feeling impassioned anymore. I wish she had the chance to rub shoulders with these three women who, in a country that doesn't always recognize women in leadership, were not looking around for approval but charging ahead in their kingdom assignments.

While I don't want anyone to serve where they are no longer called, I am not sure measuring our feelings is the right barometer for engagement. I assume Tabitha has had some days in the last forty-five years when she didn't feel like facing the battle. The testimony of her life stood out to me far above the church history books and commentaries I had been reading. This woman listened to the Lord, walked into the mission, offered herself, and stayed. God molded her this way and is honored by her obedience. She isn't asking anyone if she can or should do what she's doing; she lives fully in her gifts and will one day greet the Father, knowing she offered "help," as ezers do.

She lives fully in her gifts and will one day greet the Father, knowing she offered help, as ezers do.

These three Indian women stood out to me in a moment when I needed to take my head out of the books and position papers. I needed to *see* ezer in action, and I did, times three. She is beautiful, strong, vulnerable, and powerful. She is biblical, and we need her to keep showing up.

These living examples come from a long line of gospel-engaging women who used their resources and gave their lives to bring light into dark places. Consider a woman named Salome, mentioned at the cross (Mark 15:40) and identified as one of the women who followed Jesus. Or Joanna, the wife of Chuza, a manager of King Herod's estate or possibly his vineyard in Galilee (Luke 8:3). Both women had been ministering to Jesus' needs out of their own resources (Mark 15:41; Luke 8:1–3), so they were presumably moderately wealthy. They traveled with Jesus, at least part of the time, and it is logical to think they would have ministered to those who came to hear Him teach. Women using their resources for ministry purposes *is an old story.* It's been going on since Miriam and Esther, through Jesus' time, and now today.

So, what did the New Testament church think about these women? For the first couple of centuries, most meetings, what we would consider "churches," were held in homes. One of the first house churches gathered in a woman's house: Lydia's (Acts 16:40). A second house church met in a woman's house: Priscilla's in Ephesus (1 Corinthians 16:19). A third house church was held in a woman's house: Mary's (Acts 12:12) ... and the story goes on. We also read, "Give greetings to the brothers in Laodicea and to Nympha and to the church in her house" (Colossians 4:15 NABRE). Right in the center of the earliest records of churches were women.

Yale University New Testament professor Wayne Meeks wrote, "In four places in the Pauline letters specific congregations are designated by the phrase *hē kat' oikon* (+ possessive pronoun) *ekklēsia*, which we may tentatively translate 'the assembly at N's household.'"[9] Writer Margaret Mowczko supported the point: "Women were involved in each of these four house churches. Prisca [or Priscilla], with Aquila, hosted and led a house church in Ephesus (1 Cor. 16:19), and later in Rome (Rom. 16:3–5). Apphia was a prominent member of a house church in Colossae and is one of three people greeted individually in Philemon 1:1–2. Nympha hosted a church in her home in Laodicea and is greeted in Colossians 4:15."[10]

What did women do in those gatherings? These women were busy, not debating their position, but serving the Church as they

> taught (Acts 18:26),
> prophesized (Acts 21:9),
> served in official roles in church leadership (Romans 16:1),
> led and hosted church communities (Colossians 4:15), and
> went out to bring the message of Jesus (Romans 16:1, 7).

They followed the Great Commission to "go," "make disciples," "baptize," and "teach," and they weren't stopped, because everyone knew Jesus said so.

I remember the first time I went to Asia Minor (modern-day Turkey) to study Paul's journey. Todd and I were gifted a chance to travel to Israel and Turkey and study under Bible teacher Ray Vander Laan. We came home with dozens of stories and a journal full of insights, but one stood out more than all the others: *God is love.*

That's not what I thought I was going to come home understanding better. I thought for sure I had already learned all there was to know about *God-is-love.* Instead, I imagined learning grand insights into Paul's journeys, the house church, and maybe persecution. I thought I would get my head wrapped around geography or theology.

God-is-love most struck me when we visited Bethsaida, a small fishing village in Israel from where five of the twelve disciples hailed. I always pictured those boys coming alongside Jesus, watching his God-like miracles, hearing His God-like teachings, and then traveling after His resurrection to Asia Minor, telling the godless people about God. Wow, was I wrong.

They did all those things for sure, but when they arrived, they found the people of the Roman and Greek cultures perfectly happy with their own gods (who they believed healed and saved and provided, and for whom they built temples and hosted holiday festivals). What did the disciples have to offer these foreign cultures? They had *love.*

Jesus prepared them for it. He told them they would be known by their love. He gave them great commandments and great commissions that were all about love. And so immediately upon arrival, they began their mission. (Again, me with my uninformed ideas, believing they somehow passed around flyers, "services at 9:00 and 11:00 ...") Instead of the people coming to a church, they took the church to the people. They loved the widow and the orphan. They reached out to the slave, the hungry, and the sick. As they fleshed out this God-is-love theology, people became curious about Jesus of Nazareth and His teaching. The house churches flourished as communities began to care for one another, sharing what they had and celebrating together. *And women were right in the middle of it all.*

Extra-biblical literature carries stories of women serving throughout the early church. The African church father Tertullian (AD 160–220) described an unnamed woman prophet in his congregation who served as a counselor and healer.

> We have now among us a sister whose lot it has been to be favoured with sundry gifts of revelation, which she experiences in the Spirit by ecstatic vision amidst the sacred rites of the Lord's day in the church: she converses with angels, and sometimes even with the Lord; she both sees and hears mysterious communications; some men's hearts she understands, and to them who are in need she distributes remedies. Whether it be in the reading of Scriptures, or in the chanting of psalms, or in the preaching of sermons, or in the offering up of prayers, in all these religious services matter and opportunity are afforded to her of seeing visions.[11]

What can I learn from her example two thousand years later? I wonder ... what was it like to be her friend? Who surrounded her and encouraged her gifts? How "other" did she feel in that community, where typically men were the spiritual leaders? This ancient ezer, who "helped" both genders, sharing freely what she was given by God. He's been talking to and through women for a long time.

Also, in Italy's oldest churches, we find a lesser-known visual record of women in ministry. *Christianity Today* reported, "From around the time of the First Council of Nicaea down to the 12th century, Christians created depictions of women preaching, women marked as clergy, and even one carrying a Communion chalice, with which believers have always recalled Christ's words 'This is my blood of the covenant, which is poured out for many for the forgiveness of sins' (Matthew 26:28)."[12]

The women of the early church movement would be familiar to us. They were bold, relational, and creative. They were intentional, sensitive, and nurturing. Alongside their brothers, the church they built in their homes grew and grew and grew and grew until four centuries later, they were the dominant faith in the region. His plan works.

Questions to Consider

Who are some living ezer examples in your life?

What activities were the early church women engaged in?

What part do feelings play in your choice to engage—or not engage?

Journal

Journal how you imagine the women of the first-century church contributing to the ministry of spreading the good news. What do you think they *did*?

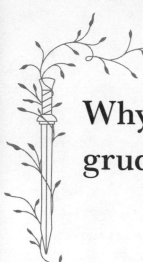

Chapter 7

Why have I held a Paul grudge all these years?

I recently volunteered with our city ministry by helping lead a cooking class for marginalized women. We used local ingredients to create "make ahead" meals they could later serve their families. Since my wheelhouse is Mexican food (residing in Mexico for fifteen years), I taught how to make taquitos, salsa, and guacamole. It was a powerful afternoon of talking about their lives while we cut and cooked. When they left, I began to clean the food-prep area and picked up some barely used water bottles to toss in the trash. I loaded the bottles into my arms but stopped short of throwing them away. *They are too heavy and will break the bag*, I thought. I walked over to the sink to drain them first.

Realizing I could kill two birds with one stone, as the water poured from the bottles, I cleaned avocado out from under my fingernails. At just that moment, one of our newer staff members walked behind me and noticed I was essentially washing my hands with purified water. He later mentioned to someone else, "Beth Guckenberger wouldn't wash her hands with city water; she had to use bottled water. I promise. I saw it with my own eyes."

When I heard about this, I laughed. He was right that he had seen me, but his understanding of what he had seen was wrong. And it was way grosser than city water, as I was partially using someone's backwash to clean my hands.

It was an honest mistake from someone who didn't know me well. I was simply misunderstood.

I need to confess that I misunderstood Paul for a long time. I respected him, studied him, and quoted him, but I wasn't sure I liked everything he said. I saw him "washing his hands with purified water," but I didn't see the context and jumped to some false conclusions.

Knowing I was going to tackle Paul's perspective on women, I asked God to help me. I knew starting with prayer would lead to a better shot at growth and not defensiveness. *What are You going to teach me here? What issues in my heart will surface? What can I see and grow from? What will I need to let go of?*

The New Testament church where Paul led grappled with all the same complexity in gender relationships that we experience today. The church was functioning in a broken world where social inequality was a common reality they experienced. They lived under the laws and customs of the Roman Empire, where for the most part, women existed as decorations and men ran the business of life. There were long-standing systems at work, and when Paul wrote to the individual churches, he addressed the society of his time and place, with the heart (of Jesus) to turn it *inside out*.

He wanted communities where love and servanthood put on display the nature of God.

In Paul's letter to Ephesus, he described marriage relationships with the cultural assumption the wife was obligated to submit to the husband (Ephesians 5:24–33). Through his turn-it-upside-down Jesus style, he admonished men to love their wives, as Christ loved the church, to love their wives as they did their own bodies. He painted a picture of mutual love and respect, which would have been shocking to the culture he was addressing. A Jewish custom for men at the time was to add to their morning prayers, "Thank You, God, for not making me a Gentile, a woman, or a slave."

He also addressed the slave under the same assumption that the slave was obligated to submit to the master (Ephesians 6:5–9). This was not an endorsement of slavery; it was an acknowledgment of the legal realities of his audience. He wasn't condoning those social inequalities; he was saying, "Jesus followers, I know we are equal. I told as much to Galatia ..."

> So in Christ Jesus, you are all children of God through faith, for all of you who were baptized into Christ have clothed yourselves with Christ. There is neither Jew nor Gentile, neither slave nor free, nor is there male and female, for you are all one in Christ Jesus. (Galatians 3:26–28)

In essence saying, "But, Church, this is the world we live in. So, marriage partners, submit to each other ... Even if our hierarchical-patriarchal culture doesn't get us, functionally, we can be equal. Slaves, within the sinful system we are stuck in, live like you are free."

There were a couple of passages I couldn't read without shaking my head. If read without context, it could lead someone to believe women should not speak aloud in Christian gatherings or teach or be in leadership over men. We know Paul didn't think that because we have plenty of examples of when he authorized women to do just these kinds of thing!

> In Acts 18:26, Priscilla discipled and instructed Apollos.
> In Acts 21:9, Philip the evangelist had four daughters who
> prophesied.
> In Romans 16:1, 7, Paul commended Phoebe as a deacon and
> Junia as an apostle.
> In Colossians 4:15, Paul sent greetings to Nympha, who had
> a house church.

So, what do the head-scratching verses mean, the ones many women either don't like or don't understand or skip entirely? Let's look at them together.

1 Corinthians 14:34–35: "Women should remain silent in the churches. They are not allowed to speak, but must be in submission, as the law says. If they want to inquire about something, they should ask their own husbands at home; for it is disgraceful for a woman to speak in the church."

1 Timothy 2:11–12: "A woman should learn in quietness and full submission. I do not permit a woman to teach or to assume authority over a man; she must be quiet."

Could it be that Paul was saying, "Women, I am so glad you appreciate the freedom to use your voice within God's house. I don't want you to be disruptive; that doesn't put God on display. The goal here isn't to be heard; it's for Him to be seen in our obedience"? It was new for women to be allowed in settings like the early church was providing, being taught by leaders. That was not something that happened in the Jewish community—religious instruction was traditionally for men only. Jesus changed all of that. Women were welcomed in, and they were likely interrupting, arguing, and talking out of turn excessively, especially when they didn't understand.

The submission and quietness Paul described in 1 Corinthians 14:34 and 1 Timothy 2:11 would not have been unique to women, as it was also the attitude men were normally expected to have while receiving religious instruction. Women were not prohibited from holding leadership positions. They were being instructed to demonstrate humility and respect for others suitable to Christian leadership (Luke 22:25–26).

I'm reminded of one specific time attending a state-mandated meeting for parents of high school athletes. I had sat through this same hour course on evaluating injury and good sportsmanship for multiple years, and so I began a side conversation with the woman next to me. I'll admit we were probably a bit disruptive, so I didn't protest when the moderator shushed us and said, "Ladies, no talking please."

He wasn't saying "only ladies can't talk." He was addressing us as the disrupters, not us as a gender.

In 1 Corinthians 11:6, Paul asked women to follow societal norms for the good name of the church. But in other passages, he requested similar things of the entire community. Earlier in the same letter, in chapter 8, Paul asked men *and* women to limit their freedom (in this case, what they ate) to promote unity in the church. First Corinthians 14 can be confusing to the modern reader, but Paul was careful to explain in verses 11–12 that men and women are mutually interdependent equals, each being the source of the other's life.

As we said at the start of this book, we are to model our behavior after Eden, when God made us ezer kenegdos. Too often in modern church politics, we try to model the third chapter of Genesis and perpetuate the fall. "It has been argued by some that God instructed men to be leaders and women to be followers for their own good at this time. But, this cannot be the case. All the consequences of human disobedience described in Gen. 3:16–18 are portrayed as entirely nega- tive. None are benevolent or instructional. Just as we are not instructed to inflict pain on birthing women, plant thorns in our gardens, or kill one another to carry out the curse in our lives, men are not instructed here to subjugate women beneath themselves."[13]

Maybe my Paul grudge isn't toward the apostle at all but more toward those who have used his words in error, holding back women from exercising their full gifts. I attended the memorial service of Steve Douglass, the former president of Campus Crusade for Christ ("Cru"), and a staff member recalled him once saying, "I don't want to stand before God one day and answer for the fact that I held back or down 50 percent of our community. Women need to be given every opportunity as their brother to fulfill the Great Commission and use their gifts." This wise pos- ture moves us forward. It's plainspoken and utterly unpolitical.

I am encouraged by examples of women throughout history who looked to God and not men. We need to tell their stories and draw strength from their legacies. Like all of us, they were brutally assaulted by the enemy, who knew what they were capable of and feared it. Their stories are more than just what they accomplished; they are testimonies of women believing in their worth.

One bold example is Aimee Semple McPherson, a woman unafraid to use her gifts of evangelism, preaching, and helps. In 1919, she began her ministry in Los Angeles by launching a series of meetings that would give her national recognition. Almost immediately, the largest American venues could not hold the crowds who gathered to hear her preach. By 1923, she dedicated Angelus Temple, which held 5,300 people. During the Depression, the Angelus Temple Commissary provided food, clothing, and other necessities to needy families without charge. In 1944, after an evening gathering of 10,000 people, Aimee tragically died of kidney failure and the effects of prescription drugs she had been taking. Today, the denomination she founded, the International Church of the Foursquare Gospel, has more than 2 million members in nearly 30,000 churches worldwide.

This is a woman who understood how to accept a spiritual assignment that outsized her. The ezer warrior learns to hold on to visions while working "with all the energy Christ so powerfully works in" her (Colossians 1:29). The Great Commission needs women, like Aimee, to see it fulfilled. Mishandling the Paul conversation is more than just managing our preferences; if we bench 50 percent of the team, there are eternal ramifications.

Mishandling the Paul conversation is more than just managing our preferences; if we bench 50 percent of the team, there are eternal ramifications.

Women need to feel they can exercise their gifts within the Church. My heart breaks for women who feel shame for their strength or hear they are following the world's ways when they lead or speak up. Church, let's follow Jesus' lead and draw courage from Paul's example by supporting women in their callings and celebrating how God designed them. If we hold women back who are called to go, make disciples, baptize, and teach, there are people who won't hear the gospel and who won't spend eternity with Jesus.

The stakes are *that* high.

Questions to Consider

Historically, what have been your feelings toward Paul's teaching?

What are some ways Paul went against his patriarchal society?

What questions do you still have about the passages addressed in this chapter?

Journal

What do you think happens when women's gifts are limited within the Church?

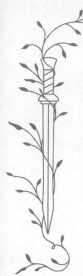

Chapter 8

When have I joined men in battle, and when have I picked one instead?

I am married to an Enneagram 8, a high D on the DISC assessment ... if those mean anything to you. Whatever instrument you are familiar with, my husband registers off the chart in leadership, assertiveness, challenge, boldness, and aggression. In the early years of our marriage, we spent many hours trying to understand how to make decisions and form an ecosystem that honored my gifts, his personality, and our Bibles. Our parents had made their own unique arrangements within their marriages.

At the time, the Church wasn't talking about it much, but when it did, the idea was reinforced that Todd had at least 51 percent of the vote. When I went looking for any books on how and when to yield to one another, their viewpoints sat on the extreme edges of the conversation: either "submit as a good Christian woman" or "never acquiesce to a man."

The question of submission: What if sometimes it made sense and other times it did not? And made sense to who—*me*? Was I supposed to only help when it felt right? What if in some areas I have more insight and at other times he does? Why do all these labels and camps and opinions leave people divided and confused? How can the next generation of women fully participate while still being uniquely female? The questions are worth the conversation, and the answer isn't to swallow what you "always thought." It isn't to act one way while thinking another. We have to humble ourselves, do the work, pray for discernment, pursue wise counsel, and live in the tension of the "now, but not yet."

Although often talked about in the context of marriage, ezer activities are not exclusive to marriage. We have a whole spiritual family to co-mission alongside. I can be an ezer to my brothers as well as my husband. One time when I was co-hosting a mission trip with my friend Brandon, we were dividing responsibilities and serving alongside a visiting team. At the end of the week, two of the participants made life-changing decisions to follow Jesus and wanted to be baptized. I had baptized lots of people at this point in my life and was the "senior" staff member between the two of us. However, Brandon played a key role in those conversations and was, in my mind, a more natural choice to lead them.

"I think you should baptize them," he started in. "I've never done it before and I want them to remember it later for how they were feeling, not how I was fumbling around, figuring it out."

"We can practice," I protested. "Plus, *you* were with them when they prayed ..." I looked at him imploringly. The rest of the conversation isn't worth recording here, just the banter of two spiritual siblings working out the logistics of a small baptism ceremony that Brandon later facilitated. I offered what I had (experience, encouragement) to him; this was the act of an ezer. Feeling my support, he stepped into the assignment; this was his act as an Adam.

Ezers offer. We encourage and take risks. When we talk about women being helpers—yes, there is an element to our helping one another and men—it's help in the sense that they couldn't do without the ezer. (Just as there are many assignments we couldn't accomplish without Adam.) Ezer as warrior implies God directly empowers, encourages, and emboldens us to do His work because He finds us worthy of the calling. There isn't a mediator; we are a direct extension of Him, a representative of Him within the kingdom of priests.

But how do we help in a way that is utterly unique? In friendship, at work, in our marriages? In a world that is confusing gender and identity, and redefining cultural norms and standards, let's consider how God builds us (biology) and instructs us (theology).

One look at any marketing campaign geared toward women and you get a sense of our diversity. Women are strong and soft. We are serious and playful. We are all the words and come in every shade. Layer onto it race, culture, background, personalities, and interests and there's no box we can neatly fit into.

In researching biblical womanhood for this project, I read articles, blogs, and books, listened to podcasts and sermons, and there are lots of mixed messages out there. Who are we?

Scientific findings show our brains are unique from men's. While these are generalities and may make you bristle if it isn't your experience, we can't break science. Some of this is how we are literally designed. A few examples:

- Men are better at performing single tasks; women are better at multitasking.
- Women are better at attention, word memory and social cognition, and verbal abilities.
- Men are better at spatial processing and sensorimotor speed.
- Women are better at fine motor coordination and retrieving information from long-term memory.
- Women are more oriented toward and have better memories of faces, while men do of things.
- Men are better at visualizing a two- or three-dimensional shape rotated in space, at correctly determining angles from the horizontal, at tracking moving objects, and at aiming projectiles.
- The female brain has more wiring in the areas that play a role in social cognition and verbal communication. That may be why we're better at empathizing with others, have a better sense of what is happening around us, and are richer in verbal descriptions.
- During activities, the male brain uses much more gray matter while the female brain uses more white matter. This difference is believed to account for the greater ability of males to focus

on a specific task to the exclusion of what's happening around them, while women are better at switching between tasks.[14]

This is just a small sampling of the research that speaks to the distinctions between women and men, and for every case that reinforces the science, there *are* exceptions. But we have an Intelligent Designer, and it honors Him when we appreciate our differences.

To continue our questions: What do we see as particularly feminine? Who gave us that idea? How does the way we judge ourselves against standards impact how we see ourselves or want others to see us?

We can wrongly assume *warrior* means "fighter," as in "fighting *against*," almost synonymous with "killer." But women are also sustainers and nurturers of life. From pregnancy to elder care, we spend our whole lives fighting *for* life, one way or another. I can testify, as can all the other women I know, of fighting for my unborn child, fighting for my sick child, fighting for my wayward teenager, fighting for my husband's heart, fighting for my parent's life.

As I write this, I wonder how well I've been an ezer. The battle between men and women can creep into even the most intimate of settings. When in marriage have I joined Todd in battle? Or started one on my own? When have I waved off his help or that of other men, or insisted on stepping in when my help wasn't needed? When have I had my eyes open to warn of future trouble and when have I been about my own agenda? This calling is a tall order, and plenty is going against a biblical execution. There's the combination of my sin, the influence of the culture, poor teaching, my temperament, and a fierce enemy.

When have I had my eyes open to warn of future trouble and when have I been about my own agenda?

Aside from a few cultures, women haven't been treated well throughout history. The once-beautiful-now-fallen Lucifer has a special hatred and design for women. Why? This enemy who was once known for beauty now hates what he can never be again. He represents death; we represent life. He is darkness; we are beautiful and light-bearing. We will spend our whole lives fighting with one hand tied behind our backs if we don't see our stories in light of the spiritual story being told in a world we cannot see. We won't understand our feminine essence (not the world's version, but the Spirit-filled, passionate-warrior version) until we understand we are loved by God and hated by His archenemy.

But God has more power in His finger (Exodus 8) than this enemy has altogether, and our unstoppable God is in pursuit of us. He wants to heal our understanding of ourselves. He wants to restore our relationships with men. He wants to redeem our relationships with other women. He wants to reconcile our relationships with our children. He wants to repair our relationships with our lovers. He wants to rescue us.

Questions to Consider

Describe a time when you were an ezer, or help, to a friend.

What differences have you noticed between men and women?

What role do you see the enemy playing in this conversation?

Journal

When has it seemed easier to pick a fight with a man than to join him?

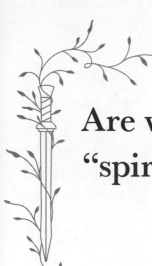

Chapter 9

Are we today still as "spirited as lions"?

In 1792, William Carey, the famous missionary to India, preached a sermon from Isaiah 54:2–3, summing up its teaching in these two important statements: "Expect great things from God" and "Attempt great things for God." This led to the formation of the Baptist Missionary Society, and Carey, at age thirty-three, proved his sincerity by volunteering to be its first missionary. Pastor and missionary Andrew Fuller had said, "There is a gold mine in India; but it seems as deep as the center of the earth; who will venture to explore it?"

"I will go down," responded William Carey, in words never to be forgotten, "but remember that you must hold the rope."[15]

How do women hold the ropes for each other and the Adams in their lives? There are many verses that highlight men as powerful, resourceful, smart, confident, and generous. And there are many that highlight women as powerful, resourceful, smart, confident, and generous too. This isn't a conversation to the exclusion of the other gender, but to the inclusion of women in some of the greatest stories ever told.

Esther, Deborah, and Mary are women whose obedience was critical to the stories in which they were highlighted. Their faith was actionable, displayed in how they walked out their callings, and provided biblical examples of courageously ezering Mordecai, Lappidoth, and Joseph. Tamar and Rahab were in circumstances they couldn't control, and yet, they used their ezer-like help to advance the kingdom, winning them a place in the genealogy of Jesus. I want to highlight passages where women were ezers—helping in ways people couldn't help themselves. This list isn't exhaustive; it's meant to be a sampling, to paint a fuller picture of women God partnered with in His story.

Women are generous. In Luke 8:1–3, we learn Jesus and the disciples had patrons, who were often wealthy women. Similarly, Paul's ministry was financed by women (Romans 16:2). A deaconess named Phoebe was identified as Paul's "patron" (ESV), or "benefactor" (NIV), a term that means "defender" or "protector."[16] She also used her money and influence to help the missionaries fulfill their calling. Others, like Priscilla (Romans 16:3–5) and Lydia (Acts 16:14–15), volunteered their homes.

I know many generous women who have started companies, administered foundations, and given of their time, talent, and dollars. I bring a couple of special women into any of my new opportunities because they cover me in many ways, what author John Rinehart calls "gospel patrons." Men are fabulous providers, and I've benefited both personally and as a missionary from their generosity, but that doesn't mean ezers haven't been given this assignment as well.

Women are strategic and ministry minded. In Romans 16:12, Paul wrote about Tryphena, Tryphosa, and Persis, who had "worked very hard in the Lord." Priscilla and Aquila were essential partners, left behind to maintain the church when Paul departed for a different city (Acts 18). In Philippians 4:2–3, Paul made it clear that both Euodia and Syntyche "labored side by side with me in the gospel together with Clement and the rest of my fellow workers" (ESV). These women in the thick of things strategized, made leadership decisions, and handled tremendous responsibility.

Women are teachers. We know women can teach. They teach us how to eat, how to treat others, how to read and write in school ... They possess the skills and the capacity. It only makes sense God would use this ability to share the most important information of all: spiritual instruction. Luke 2:36–38 introduces Anna the prophetess as a woman who served the Lord by staying in the temple and worshipping. She would also teach the people and "speak of him to all who were waiting for the redemption of Jerusalem" (ESV). Timothy received training in the doctrines of the faith from his godly grandmother Lois and his mother, Eunice (2 Timothy 1:5). We know this meant instruction in "the sacred writings," which made him "wise for salvation through faith in Christ Jesus" (2 Timothy 3:15 ESV). Again, let's remember the Great Commission, given to both genders: "Go, make disciples, baptize, and teach" (see Matthew 28:19).

Women are kind. In Romans 16, we read about Rufus, a man with a remarkable mother (and father; he carried Jesus' cross). Paul said she was like the adoptive church mother, and like a mother to him as well (Romans 16:13). Tabitha was likely the same kind of woman, "full of good works and acts of charity" (Acts 9:36 ESV). Aren't some ezers just remarkable? They've fully embodied their gifts and passed them around, lending authority and significance to the work they endeavor. That's how I imagine Rufus's mother—someone who wielded influence and shared it with her husband and son. Ezer isn't just a list of activities I have the privilege to execute; being a suitable helper is essential to how God made me. It pours out in every interaction and influences my very core.

Women are brave. An interesting biblical character named Junia is found in Romans. Some people thought because she was powerful and an apostle, she must have been a man. For a season in biblical scholarship, they changed her name to the masculine Junias. However, for hundreds of years now, we've acknowledged her as a woman and as an early church leader, right alongside Paul. In Romans 16:7, she worked so closely with Paul that she suffered as a "fellow prisoner" (ESV). That's extreme commitment, and it proves that Paul didn't mind having women at his side during a dangerous mission for the gospel. He ended Romans with warm and personal greetings, deeply thankful for the service and sacrifice of women. We don't have the words Junia shared; we only know she was an important part of spreading the gospel.

Commenting on Romans 16:7, John Chrysostom (AD 347–407), bishop of Constantinople, praised Junia as an outstanding apostle: "Greet Andronicus and Junia ... who are outstanding among the apostles."[17]

To be an apostle is something great! But to be outstanding among the apostles—just think what a wonderful song of praise that is! They were outstanding on the basis of their works and virtuous actions. Indeed, how great the wisdom of this woman must have been that she was even deemed worthy of the title of apostle.

Chrysostom also praised the service of other Christian women. Reflecting on Paul's greeting of Mary in Romans 16:6, he wrote:

> A woman again is honored and proclaimed victorious! Again, are we men put to shame. Or rather, we are not put to shame only, but have even an honor conferred upon us. For an honor we have, in that there are such women among us, but we are put to shame, in that we men are left so far behind by them.... For the women of those days were more spirited than lions.[18]

We could continue this list with women who are as spirited as lions and faithful like Hannah, wise like Deborah, leaders like Miriam ... To be fair, these things are true about men too. They are generous, strategic, ministry-minded, teachers, kind, and brave. Again, I am not saying women are these things to the exclusion of men. We can have these characteristics *as well* as our brothers. The kinds of questions we are asking aren't because we lack faith; they are precisely because we *have* faith. A warrior's life is risky, dangerous at times, grueling most days, and definitely not comfortable. Ezer is disciplined, focused, always ready, and fiercely strong; this is a beautiful image of a woman.

God is asking His *ezers* to engage in the world: brave and kind, teachers and strategic thinkers, generous, and all the rest. Sometimes we get paid for it, and sometimes we don't. Whether we work inside or outside the home, we can wholeheartedly agree women are working, contributing, and leading.

This arrangement can cause complications. Sometimes it stresses us out. *Do we go right or left? Work here or there? Are we working too much? Too loudly? Too hard? To the detriment of our children? To the shame of our husbands? To the cost of our sanity?*

I am learning to say to myself, the Lord, and anyone watching, *I am simply doing the best I can.* This means some days I am killing it and my work benefits. And some days I am dropping more plates than I have hands, and that's okay too.

If you have children, it can be guilt-inducing to feel like you want to accomplish goals outside of child-rearing. And while my children are my priority, they aren't the only calling I have. Overcoming "mom guilt" requires me to be present when I am present with them (parenting instead of managing). I turn down the phone and curb my multitasking tendencies. My kids aren't projects; they are people who need eye contact, to be heard, and to have someone curious about their lives. Being heard by someone who has given you their full attention without judgment is profoundly healing. This is what Jesus does for us, and may we be His earthly example. How we talk to our kids influences how they will talk to themselves later. This is critical work and our unique calling as their parents.

> **If you have children, it can be guilt-inducing to want to accomplish goals outside of child-rearing. While my children are my priority, they aren't the only calling I have.**

However, taking on too much responsibility for my children—emotionally and otherwise—works against healthy spiritual engagement. I have to believe that God is their primary parent. *He* encourages, convicts, guides, and counsels (and uses me sometimes to do it). It is critical I teach them to listen to God. He never leaves them and can be the voice in their heads telling them to go or stop. I can get in trouble when I think in my absence, they are "alone." He is always with them, and the more I can do to foster their attachment to Him, the better. What rules their hearts will influence their behavior, so my work is engaging in deep heart work with them, not behavior management.

Ultimately, with any work I do, I trust I am setting an example to my family in how to engage: I want them to see me offering my hands and gifts to a broken world. They are the most significant part of my life, but they aren't my whole life. As my children have gotten older, it's been important for me to be honest with them when I find myself out of balance. They will spend their lives in the same dance, and the more vulnerably I can share my journey, the more chance I have for discipleship.

Some women are doing this on their own as single parents, working and caring with supernatural glory strength (Colossians 1). We need to come alongside these sisters and offer ourselves as liberally as we can. Some of us are in two-parent households and *still* think it's all on us. Recognizing the role of "Adam" in our ecosystem means relying on him to share responsibilities. When I do, it's a gift to our house, not a failure on my part. As women, we can put pressure on ourselves, but the truth is, our teamwork is an example of how modern households work. We are two planks propped up against each other.

It's not easy balancing household responsibilities and outside work (both kingdom and otherwise), but getting my head in the right place helps my heart when it struggles with guilt. The word *balance* is unforgiving—as if nothing can ever fall. I prefer the word *rhythm*, which means some days are fast and some slow, and managing that tension is the reality of life with work you care about and kids you love. On the days when I struggle, I hope sharing it, rather than pretending, shows my humanity. Together, we can confess where there have been missteps and misunderstandings and ask Jesus for the strength to do better tomorrow. I pray the result is a marriage and a family who listens to each other, who have the right words and experiences to foster connection and an identity in line with a biblical worldview.

Questions to Consider

In the biblical examples listed in this chapter, which most resonated with you?

What does your self-talk sound like?

How much does guilt play a part in your decisions to engage?

Journal

What makes you as spirited as a lion?

Chapter 10

What if warrioring just isn't me?

"I may be in the minority," wrote a friend from college, "but I don't want to fight. This idea we are supposed to be warriors doesn't resonate with me. I want to care for someone, not do battle with them. What if *ezer* as warrior doesn't fit me?"

To some, helping, fighting, and warrioring mean bold steps, advocation, tough love, and big risks. It's hard not to confuse noise with impact. But warrioring can also mean intercessory prayer, unrelenting service, and quiet sacrifice. It can be a fierce kind of battle that asks for costly, consistent love. Some of the best ezering I've ever seen has come from women who love prodigals. They could be sons, but also friends, coworkers, parents, and siblings. This is relentless work: living your faith with integrity, extending grace, and allowing someone to face consequences without "I told you so." And the prayer—the endless prayers over every day and every risk. If prayers built visible muscles, these women would look like some of our fiercest soldiers.

Lara Croft: Tomb Raider was my friend's favorite movie. She identified with the battle-ready character, and whenever she had to do something hard, we'd call her "Tomb Raider." It was code for "you can do it," even if she didn't want to do whatever she was facing. I never saw those movies, but I got the impression Lara Croft never backed down and could be counted on to defend you. While that makes for a good movie, it's not what the Bible means by *ezer*.

Not all warriors love to fight, but this doesn't mean they aren't "in the fight." Their weapons, for example, might be service, listening, or prayer. Our personalities, giftings, backgrounds, birth order, and culture all factor into how we offer help. Mother Teresa's ministry, which earned her a Nobel Peace Prize in 1979, was reaching out to lepers, addicts, and the Untouchable class in India.

Not all warriors love to fight, but this doesn't mean they aren't "in the fight."

I saw a news conference from Mother Teresa's visit to the United States years ago. She was hosted by First Lady Hillary Clinton, arguably the most powerful woman in the world. Mother Teresa was revered, although she had no title or political position. It was fascinating to watch the room revolve around Mother Teresa, as the moon revolves around earth. It seemed visibly uncomfortable to Mrs. Clinton, who kept trying to redirect the spotlight to herself. I don't fault her; that would have been her experience in almost every other room she entered and must have felt odd to be usurped by this diminutive woman. It has stuck in my memory all these years in part because of the striking contrast in their perceived power. Mother Teresa was a powerful ezer, but in an utterly countercultural way.

How can we honor the quiet obedience of ezers like this all over the world? Women who are holding up the other side of the plank of their partners and friends? Who are staying in the fight when it's easier to run away? Who are looking out for the interest of others while their culture roars for them to be self-absorbed? Who are in over their heads and still not quitting? We don't have to fit in a mold, follow a course, or imitate anyone other than Jesus. Just look for people and respond to what we see.

The work for me is to have my eyes up, looking around instead of focusing on my own day or needs. When I am on the lookout for others, what do I notice? A recent study reported in the *New York Post* stated the average American spends a minimum of six hours a day looking at a screen.[19] We are looking at all kinds of people and circumstances, but what are we seeing?

I have a neighbor who is going through a divorce, and it's obvious—moving trucks, front-porch conflicts, and children not always in residence. I see it happening, but I haven't done much to get involved. The Hebrew word *ra'ah* means "to see," but it also means "to respond to a need." Embedded in its definition is the challenge if we don't do anything about what we are looking at, can we claim to have seen it?

In Acts 3, Peter and John went together to the temple at the hour of prayer:

> Now a man who was lame from birth was being carried to the temple gate called Beautiful, where he was put every day to beg from those going into the temple courts. When he saw Peter and John about to enter, he asked them for money. Peter looked straight at him, as did John. Then Peter said, "Look at us!" (Acts 3:2–4)

The Greek word translated as "looked straight at him" is also translated as "rivet your eyes on, look intensely, do a double take." He didn't just look; he look-*looked*.

Peter and John would have been to the temple for prayer many times over the years as this man had been sitting there, waiting. What made them see him this time? What makes us look-look at something we have previously ignored?

I like to think Peter saw this man for his potential, as he went on to heal him in the next verses. Peter wasn't defining him by his circumstances; he saw a man with Spirit-filled eyes. What would happen if we looked at people for their potential and not their labels? What if we looked beyond what has happened to them and saw them as God does: created, valued, loved, forgiven, chosen, and special? What happens to us as people when we stop looking altogether?

I've been trying to take a moment—it's all it takes—to look in the eyes of whoever is ringing me up in the store or bringing me a refill at the table. I don't know what it does for them, but for me, it reminds me the world is full of creations, hearts wrapped up in bodies that are curious about why they were created. We're all looking for connection. Can that shape how I look-look? I am hoping it makes me more apt to be battle ready should this ezer get called up to the field. Otherwise, I too easily default to laziness or selfishness and miss an opportunity to fight.

Jesus' Spirit-filled eyes see us as we were created to be. God knows every day the world may "like" a picture on our social media but never see us. They may notice what's happening in our homes but never offer to help. They may pass us by and never do a double take. God is different. He promises He sees us. "For the LORD sees not as man sees: man looks on the outward appearance, but the LORD looks on the heart" (1 Samuel 16:7 ESV).

Peter tells us, in 1 Peter 2:9, we are God's priests. A priest's chief responsibility is to show others what God is like. We can't *just* be recipients of His grace and goodness; we are also to be conduits or vessels of that goodness to others. All Christ followers have a calling, and I don't mean the particulars of where we sense God asking us to be or serve. His larger mission is for us to put Him on display. When we do, we are acting as we were made. This is the work of an ezer.

When someone interacts with a priest, a Christ follower, they should know more about God after the exchange. Maybe they understand His generosity, His sensitivity, His truth, or His grace. Whatever it is, it's the one task He has left us with: *represent Me through your actions to a lost world.* Because we have been seen by God, we are to *look-look* at others.

To be seen means someone:

- knows where your bruises are (and is careful to not hurt you)
- hears your dreams (and wants them to happen for you)

- celebrates the wins in your life (even if they have nothing to do with them)
- grieves your losses with you (simply because you are sad)
- keeps your confidence (and demonstrates trustworthiness)
- touches base (indicating their presence in your life is important)

The Bible teaches us God saw us before we were born (Psalm 139), and "the eyes of the LORD range throughout the earth to strengthen those whose hearts are fully committed to him" (2 Chronicles 16:9). It's He who sees us. He knows the bruises, hears our dreams, celebrates our wins, grieves our losses, keeps our confidence, and is always present. He never fails us, never tires of us, and never forgets. His kind of seeing us means He will respond to our need (for grace, mercy, patience, joy, wisdom, and love), and from that kind of attention, we can pour out onto others. Life on earth is hard because we are in the "now, but not yet." We have an inkling things could be good, might get better, or were once good, but we don't *really* know. If we use our energy trying to stay comfortable or keeping things convenient, then we'll end up sorely disappointed. The richest moments in life can be when we run out and He stretches down to make up the difference.

When I posted on my social media platforms the question "What is your reaction to being a warrior?" one woman responded, "I might be in the minority, but the idea of being called to be a warrior, in addition to everything else I juggle as a woman, is a burden I don't have the energy to take on." I understand where she's coming from; it can feel like already impossible burdens are placed on us.

Be strong, yet gentle ... carry responsibilities, but trust God with the outcome ... be beautiful, consistent, content, strong, and creative—the list keeps going. On top of all that, *be on the front lines?*

Forget it.

God is gracious with us when we don't feel like fighting. We are His, and there isn't anyone who understands our limitations and our needs more than He does. We have nothing to prove. That doesn't mean that life isn't hard and we won't be asked to do more than we think ourselves capable.

In the C. S. Lewis book *Prince Caspian*, Aslan asks the prince if he feels sufficient to take up the kingship of Narnia.

"I—I don't think I do, Sir," said Caspian. "I'm only a kid."

"Good," said Aslan. "If you had felt yourself sufficient, it would have been a proof that you were not."[20]

Questions to Consider

What does fight look like in your life?

What role did a woman play in your early faith life?

Who have you look-looked at?

Journal

When does self-sufficiency end for you and asking God for help begin?

Chapter 11

What does it mean to co-mission alongside men we aren't married to?

I have been asking myself, God, and others, what does it mean to be an ezer to *all* people? Not just my husband, but also my neighbor, coworker, dear friend, and brother-in-law. We typically think of the Genesis 2 passage in reference to marriage, but our image isn't only reflected when we are married. We are helpers and warriors from the moment His Spirit lives within us (Ezekiel 36:27; Romans 8:11), regardless of our marital status. So, what does that look like? Did God make me a helper to *everyone*? If not everyone, then to whom?

Even a basic understanding of the character of God recognizes His love for *all* women, married or single. He had stories to tell through single women like Dorcas, Rahab, Esther, the widow at Zarephath, Lydia, Martha, Anna, and many more. So, married or not, how do we offer our strength and help to others? What does God think of *me*, not associated with my job, marital status, or any role I fulfill? And would the answer to that question help me understand how I engage with the rest of the world?

We hold to many common beliefs as Christians that hurt the body of Christ. We live in a culture as a church that idolizes marriage, which causes several unintended consequences.

- A belief that a woman's calling, or mission, only starts once she is married.
- A belief that women can only help or serve other women.
- A belief by some that men and women are unable to be friends without romantic entanglements.

When we as a Church succumb to the over-sexualization of our culture, we miss out on genuine friendship out of fear that the other will make us fall. Aimee Byrd, author of *Why Can't We Be Friends? Avoidance Is Not Purity*, said that "when Christians see their brother or sister as an object of temptation, they often feel anxious about 'ordinary acts of kindness and business' with a person of the other sex. When we instead regard one another as temptations, as means merely of gratifying sexual desires, or as threats to our image, and we do not regard one another honorably as brothers and sisters, we are not loving deeply."[21]

The Bible is full of language that positively sets up men and women as spiritual siblings. Ordinary acts of kindness and business can be encouragement, exhortation, intercession, sharing meals, assignments, complementing gifts, challenging one another, etc. Jesus Himself had sister relationships with women in His community. He accepted invitations to eat with them, talked unaccompanied, engaged in debates and discussions, allowed women to express affection for Him, and had other encounters with his spiritual sisters, establishing a new model for first-century Church interactions. While some brothers and sisters have unique situations that call for extraordinary boundaries, most of the body can enjoy healthy interactions in ways that don't threaten our message but enhance it.

Ezering, helping, extends to the whole body of Christ, and we are to be on the lookout for opportunities to fight alongside our sisters *and* brothers. Even Paul assumed and insisted brothers and sisters could engage in joint ministry without romantic engagement. Think of what he wrote in Romans 16:1–2: "I commend to you our sister Phoebe, a deacon of the church in Cenchreae. I ask you to receive her in the Lord in a way worthy of his people and to give her any help she may need from you, for she has been the benefactor of many people, including me."

And later in verse 12, he wrote, "Greet my dear friend Persis, another woman who has worked very hard in the Lord." In both cases, he was modeling men and women working together with their unique perspectives and gifts, fully reflecting God's character. I want to trust God will use me to share with others what He first gave me: insight, provision, or any number of good gifts. As recipients with hands and hearts full, we can be resources whom God delights in deploying to all people, not just our husbands, but also our coworkers, friends, unchurched neighbors, brothers-in-law, and on goes the endless list.

The purity culture I grew up in within the church wrapped our gender and sexuality in a healthy dose of fear. It emphasized the dangerous consequences and potential pain of sexual sin. Talking about male-female friendships in the context of this purity standard created a shame dynamic in an area that already had a great deal of potential for shame. When there are only two options for your behavior—right or wrong—the outcome is inevitably pride or shame. So, to prevent failure, we created great distances between "men's groups" and "women's groups" and took every opportunity to separate the genders, instead of modeling or teaching healthy ways for them to work together and maintain friendships.

> **We don't need to fear men, and they don't need to fear us. We have the Holy Spirit in us, and He can be trusted to guide, encourage, warn, convict, and lead us as we co-labor alongside them.**

Ezers, we don't need to fear men, and they don't need to fear us. We have the Holy Spirit in us, and He can be trusted to guide, encourage, warn, convict, and lead us as we co-labor alongside them. The best thing we can offer is our well-tended soul and our tender spirit, wise to the ways of evil and innocent in our motives to serve.

I welcomed a group who had traveled from the US to our home in Mexico, where they would serve for a weeklong mission trip. They were dressed like a million bucks, not the typical attire for day one of a mission trip. "Do you think someone told them they were coming to a timeshare?" I murmured to another staff member.

A man, clearly in charge and carrying a big bag of passports, was the last to step off the bus. "Here you go." He thrust the bag into my hands. "They are all yours." (I wasn't sure if he meant the passports or the people.)

"Hi, welcome to Back2Back," I said to him, curious how badly his travel day must have gone to put him in this mood. "How can I help you get settled?"

"I am already at my wit's end with this group. I can't believe we got anyone to come. I'm on staff with the church, and this is my last official week. Starting when we get back, I'll be the pastor of our new urban church plant. We've been trying to get volunteers all year, and no one will help. But advertise a mission trip to sunny Mexico and look at the response." He gestured in the general area of his team.

I was not sure what to expect after that introduction, but I was pleasantly surprised when the team pitched in during the week and engaged in new activities, ate new foods, and made new friends. By the last day, I was encouraged by their bravery and newly formed community. It had been a special time of challenge and growth for us all.

A couple of months later, I was in their city to share at their church. After the services, we gathered for a meal. As was our custom on the trip, I circled them up and asked how life had been since they'd been back: What had they been learning?

"Go on, tell her ...," encouraged the pastor who had accompanied them, joining us for lunch from his new church.

"I drive the bus for the new church plant," one of them started.

"I'm there too. I volunteer for their Wednesday children's program," shared another.

"I am a Sunday school teacher, and now my family worships there full-time," said the next one.

Round the circle we went, each one sharing where God had led them to engage in their community after their return.

"What happened?" I asked.

One lady spoke up, "I didn't realize I had anything to offer. I didn't realize I had anything in common with ... *others*. Once I saw I could do, you know, all of *that*, so far away from home, with people so different than me, then suddenly it seemed doable here."

There were quiet nods of affirmation all around me, and I learned an important lesson that day. The biggest obstacle to offering "help" is thinking that we have nothing to offer or that we have nothing in common with those we want to help. To make room for God to stir a calling to ezer, they had to do some spring cleaning, removing untested theories and outright lies that had accumulated in their hearts and minds like trash in the back seat of a car.

There is much at stake in this battle between the kingdoms of dark and light, and we need all hands on deck. We need women of all ages and stages of maturity reaching up to Jesus, into their spiritual communities, and out to the world that is still lost. We need to hold on to the truth and each other as we engage in the oldest of stories: God's kids doing God's work in God's world.

> It is a world of magic and mystery, of deep darkness and flickering
> starlight. It is a world where terrible things happen and wonderful
> things too. It is a world where goodness is pitted against evil, love
> against hate, order against chaos, in a great struggle where often it
> is hard to be sure who belongs to which side because appearances
> are endlessly deceptive. Yet for all its confusion and wildness, it
> is a world where the battle goes ultimately to the good, who live

happily ever after, and where in the long run everybody, good and evil alike, becomes known by his true name.[22]

This mission into "a world of magic and mystery, of deep darkness and flickering starlight" is not limited to women who marry or those who bear children. There are good stories yet to be told, and we war against an unseen but very real enemy. He wants to ruin us because he knows that hurting us will hurt God, and that's his goal.

Ezer isn't supposed to minimize herself when a man is around, or only offer part of herself. We need *all* ezers to bring *all* they have to bear—strength, insight, gifts, discernment, experience, wisdom, prayer—because 1 John 3:8 says, "The reason the Son of God appeared was to destroy the devil's work." We are called to partner with Him in that work, so we must keep showing up. If we limit married women to offering help only to their spouses, we pave the way for the enemy to gain more ground. We need all women to offer all their gifts to whomever God leads them.

God created His daughters to be ezer-warriors alongside His sons, whether single or married, young or old, new in faith or old saints. He knows how ezer is created, what she is capable of, and where she is called. He sends her to break man's loneliness by passionately walking and fighting alongside him. And he needs everything she brings to their mission.

Questions to Consider

What do you have in common with those you feel called to help?

What unintended consequences do you see from the Church idolizing marriage?

What do you think would need to change, if anything, for men and women to be friends?

Journal

What barriers do you see to women and men co-missioning?

Chapter 12

How do women come for one another?

"Toni, I have a favor to ask."

"Anything. Name it," she said.

I sighed in relief. I knew she was the right person to call. Toni is a ministry partner at a Houston church that supports Back2Back's work with orphaned and vulnerable children.

"My sister-in-law, Sara, who is suffering from colorectal cancer, is coming to Houston to seek treatment. She'll be there for a month or three ... we don't know. I am looking for any resources you might know of ... someone with an extra car, maybe an over-the-garage apartment for them ... Can you ask around and see if anything pops up?" By the time I said the last sentence, I was crying. Sara's fight against cancer was heartbreaking to watch and the idea that I could do *anything* to help was meaningful to me.

"For sure. Our church has a ministry set up just for this kind of need. We have condos near the hospital and people who minister to those who come into town during this vulnerable stage in their treatment. Let me see what I can do."

The tears fell silently then, and again now, as I remember how I felt on that call. This was the Church acting at its best.

Within a couple of hours, Toni had used her network and resources to secure housing, a car, meals, and airport pickups, and all this for two people she hadn't met and didn't attend her church. It was the very definition of *ezer*: offering help for someone who can't provide for themselves. Sara never got healthy enough for the treatment in Houston, but I will never forget how it felt to have someone *come* for her. Toni and her team continued to reach out to my brother after Sara's death, sending packages for their children and texting prayers. This group of women ezered him; they heard of a need and sought to meet it. This is what we do, we come *for* ... When we study the women of the Bible, we get the impression it's feminine to go in, say yes, offer, risk, and extend ourselves.

One time I arrived to speak at a conference after having a bad fall on ice. I had a concussion and visible stitches on my face. I joked at the beginning, wanting to disarm anyone who was distracted by my appearance. Immediately, and after my talk, I was rushed on the stage—by who? The women. Women came because they know how to offer care. They offered oils, pills, water, prayer ... And I didn't even know them.

I could share many examples of women coming for those they love—and for strangers. I've seen women care for neighbors, in-laws, foster children, coworkers ... Why do we care so well? Because it's in our nature.

I was sitting in a leadership conference, listening to Jackie Green of the Hobby Lobby founding family, being interviewed on their work with the Museum of the Bible. She talked about the season she spent visiting donors and curating the content that's now on display in Washington, DC. During her hundreds of dinners with strangers, she had found an easy way to start a conversation was to ask, "Tell me about your faith journey ..." She testified the answers usually had a common denominator: a woman. People shared about their mothers, grandmothers, a neighbor lady, their Sunday school teachers, women who initiated taking them to church, who listened to their stories, who shared their lives with them, and who came for them.

We have different motives for giving. I can give out of the pureness of my heart, knowing I was first cared for by God. I can give out of selfish motives because, in giving, I hope to gain something in return. Or I can give because, in my brokenness, I think I need to earn something. The difference isn't in the act but in my motive.

We live our best ezer-selves when we give out of the abundance of what we have received as His child. But we can't wait to engage until we are healed and know the motives behind our "coming for." Jesus invites us to live wholeheartedly now, and in the exchange of emptying and refilling, we'll find our healing along the way. Not everyone understands us when we live with our light on and we come *for* someone. It's tempting to turn down our light when others react negatively to it. I have wrestled with the feeling I can be "too much" and others would be more comfortable if I just "calmed down," but that thinking isn't biblical. He made me, and I need to live with my whole heart on display.

Author Marianne Williamson wrote:

> Our deepest fear is not that we are inadequate. Our deepest fear is that we are powerful beyond measure. It is our light, not our darkness, that most frightens us. We ask ourselves, "Who am I to be brilliant, gorgeous, talented, and fabulous?" Actually, who are you not to be? You are a child of God. Your playing small doesn't serve the world. There's nothing enlightened about shrinking so that other people won't feel insecure around you. We were born to manifest the glory of God that is within us. And as we let our light shine, we unconsciously permit other people to do the same. As we are liberated from our fear, our presence automatically liberates others.[23]

At the heart of an ezer is the call to come forth. As I asked women on social media to recount how other women have come for them, I heard hundreds of stories of women serving each other during seasons of sickness, adoption, job loss, and transition. I heard about acts of service (meals, childcare), stories of ministry (sending verses, coming to pray), and many examples of generosity (making room for and advocating for one another). Women who didn't wait to be invited but came in on that white horse. Women who patched up emotional, spiritual, and physical wounds. Women who listened, held each other accountable, shared wisdom, kept confidences, and celebrated another's victory. There were mothers-in-law and bosses. Neighbors, sisters, strangers, pastors ...

At the heart of an ezer is the call to come forth.

The testimonies of ezers helping both men and women in their lives made me think of something Kelly Brown wrote to me:

> *Warrior* seems to be more fitting and empowering for the role of women. *Helper* sounds like when I ask my daughter to be my kitchen helper to make cookies, and I'm certainly still running that show and having her do the simple tasks she is less likely to mess up. Warrior women lay themselves down on the line daily to fight for those they love. At the end of the day, when we may feel exhausted from work or parenting or sitting with someone through hard times and praying fervently ... the idea of reflecting on your day as an exhausted *helper* sounds as if someone worked you ragged. The idea of an exhausted *warrior* brings feelings of pride and achievement and honor along with the anticipation of well-earned rest.

Questions to Consider

How have you experienced women coming for you?

When is a time you've battled for another woman?

How does understanding your identity strengthen your faith journey?

Journal

When you shrink back from offering something to another, is it because you fear you are too much or too little?

Chapter 13

What does the concept of ezer do within the mystery of marriage?

"Marriage is the sanctuary of the heart. You have been entrusted with the heart of another human being. Whatever else your life's great mission will entail, loving and defending this heart next to you is part of your great quest."[24]

John Eldredge, *Love and War*

When we see an animal in creation do what it's designed to do—fly, swim, pollinate, hunt—we are in awe. It's the same with women. When we do what we were created to do—nurture, battle, give life—it's stirring. A strong woman makes a man stronger, not weaker. They offer and come for, they risk and fight alongside. They arouse men (not always sexually) in an awakening sense. The magic that happens between Adam and Eve is closely connected to the real and metaphorical application of being "naked and unafraid." This mystery of marriage is equal parts vulnerability, strength, offer, and connection.

Real love is unselfish; there's enough room inside a healthy relationship for a man to be as masculine as he's meant to be, while a woman is simultaneously her full expression of femininity. Neither steps on or changes the other; we can be ourselves without minimizing the other. There is no pouting or competition in this kind of mature love. No games or manipulation, no controlling or withholding. It requires putting the other person's interests first, even when the world screams to take care of yourself at all costs. When an ezer loves her Adam like this and is similarly loved, momentum takes over. They can either initiate or respond to that love and what happens next in the mystery of our intelligent design. Add chemistry, and now they are drawn to each other. When they disagree, this magnet pulls them to the other side of the fight. It gets better and deeper over time.

A marriage aided by ezer, or help, is infused with honor like grease on a hinge. It just moves better, is smoother. The subtle difference it speaks to is "I am helping you because you are mine" instead of "I am helping you because you are helpless." Honor is critical, and in its absence, resentment and contempt can creep in. Honor preserves relational intimacy. I must be healthy enough to let Todd be himself, without wanting to femininize his responses so they feel more familiar. I will never understand some parts of his maleness, but I don't have to in order for me to respect them and him. The same is true for him. He doesn't always get why and how I do, say, or prioritize things, but it's not his job to make me more like him. His responsibility is to make an emotionally safe environment for my spiritually healthy self-expression.

When women are empathetic and verbally affirming, we lift up, encourage, bear with one another, and call out the best in the men of our lives. When Todd feels seen, respected, and honored, he is the most *man* I've known him to be. There isn't second-guessing or possession, just the confident freedom you feel when someone loves you and you love them back.

Mature ezer-Adam love gets over *it*—whatever the "it" is. And each couple knows their thing. Part of holding up Todd's plank is my not reminding him of past mistakes or bringing up what makes me feel powerful so I can make him feel weak. (I don't know why that's ever an attractive option. It never works, and usually burns the house down.) Letting go of an offense is seeing him as my fellow traveler in life and not my adversary. We are each in our own blockbuster movie, and somehow in that context, God thought my life would benefit his and vice versa, so He blended our plots together. When it's good, it's a "1 + 1 = more than 2" kind of scenario. When it's bad, there are subtraction symbols, and it feels like everyone loses.

The Bible teaches us authentic love isn't threatened and should be protected; it's heady and forever. Not heady in the sense you are somebody's whole world; we should never be the other person's whole world—that's obsession. But somewhere between independent and codependent is a healthy interdependency that combines spiritual, emotional, sexual, relational, and social energy into something supernatural. That's what needs to be protected, because the world doesn't understand it and our nature fights against it. Add selfishness, spiritual warfare, and other shiny apples, and it's a miracle ezer and Adam co-mission at all.

> # Somewhere between independent and codependent is a healthy interdependency that combines spiritual, emotional, sexual, relational, and social energy into something supernatural.

There is not much about men I intuitively get. I'm not supposed to; he is *other*. We have to listen well while giving the other the benefit of the doubt. Everything I know, I've learned because I've been curious and admired how men are made. I am positive Todd understood very little about women when we got married. Sure, he knew how we looked, but it's been a steady diet of good conversation and constant observation that has led him to "get" this ezer and others.

Somewhere around year ten of our marriage, we realized our everyday interactions were becoming increasingly transactional and less intimate in nature. If we weren't talking, thinking, or acting intimate throughout the day, we weren't going to suddenly feel that way when we were alone. To mitigate where this was headed, toward more of a partnership than a marriage, we decided to set apart two hours every day to just be together without competing roles (no laundry, emailing, working, parenting, house managing, etc.). For us, it takes place from 9:00 to 11:00 every night, and I can testify this is the deepest breath of my day.

It felt radical twenty years ago when we began, but today, this time together is mission critical. It's how we grew up together and exchanged ideas, dreams, and opinions, as well as sorted out conflicts, callings, and decisions. We've found that just making space to connect has led to lots of ... well, *connecting*. Now married for thirty years, we enjoy each other sexually more than ever. I feel like that's *not* the message going out these days. In the movies, online, or in magazines, the memo is young love is passionate and old love is stale. I've found it to be quite the opposite.

The Bible encourages us to be passionate. In Song of Songs, connection with Adam is described as responsive (4:16), adventurous (7:11–13), expressive (1:16; 2:3), uninhibited (6:13–7:8), and sensuous (5:10–16). I wish the Church talked about this more. In a world where relationships are dissolving all around us, this feels like an important conversation. Used correctly, sexual intimacy is like cement connecting two people. Used as a weapon, or simply a toy, it causes soul scars that take real work to heal, and that's only when people are game for that process.

God made sex for more than procreation, and more than mechanics. He created hormones and nerves, emotions, and sensory receptors so we'd enjoy each other and stick together. There are plenty of activities *anyone* can do with Todd—work, play a game, converse, create something, fight—but there is only one person the Bible says he can be intimate with: *me*.

Song of Solomon 2:15 says, "Catch the foxes for us, the little foxes that are ruining the vineyards, while our vineyards are in blossom" (NASB). The vineyard represents our bodies, and while they might enjoy being in "blossom," there are foxes always threatening to shut us down. Some foxes are innocent, like busyness or fatigue, while others may require more work to get rid of, like body image, expectations, hurt, fear, and shame.

I used to think I was supposed to hide my foxes from Todd and always put my best foot forward, but I have learned that sharing my foxes with him allows him to fight alongside me (cultivating intimacy and vulnerability). The result? We are on a mission to hunt together what is hindering the other from a full expression of our shared love. That is a far cry from the two-dimensional version of sex the world offers, which is more about taking from the other what pleases you. It's the difference between a microwavable pizza-flavored Hot Pocket and a homemade, fire-grilled pizza made for you in the heart of Italy. They aren't even in the same category, even though they're advertised as the same flavor.

I have some fellow ezers with whom I have given permission to cheer me on in this area. They ask hard questions and challenge me to grow my box. By "box" I mean the rigid parameters I put around myself and Todd in this part of our lives. If our boxes don't grow, we are at real risk of coming together out of obligation, or to get relief, or as exercise, and that's not how this gift was designed to be experienced. It's a dynamic (as in growing) expression of intimacy that is simultaneously life-giving, vulnerable, connecting, and passionate. Anything less than this should not be acceptable. To grow our boxes, we must pray about what's inside them, learn about it, and talk to each other. It's worth the fight, ezer, to come for him and with him together like this.

Questions to Consider

If you are married, what role has honor played in your relationship?

If you are not married, have you seen an example of a marriage where the man and the woman honor their differences?

Is your relationship independent, codependent, or interdependent?

Journal

When in your marriage have you experienced intimacy as it was designed?

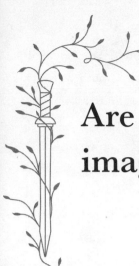

Chapter 14

Are we made in the image of a male God?

Jesus came to earth in the form of a man. God taught us to pray in Matthew 6:9, "Our Father in heaven, hallowed be your name ..." Isaiah 54:5 teaches, "For your husband is your Maker, whose name is the LORD of armies; and your Redeemer is the Holy One of Israel, who is called the God of all the earth" (NASB).

I am not trying to feminize God. I am, however, trying to reconcile the truth that women came from *somewhere*, and God claims we are made in His image (Genesis 1:27), so what part of Him is the stuff we are made of?

One year on Mother's Day, I was thinking about being a mother. If I am made in the image of God, then all we celebrate and honor about mothers we should celebrate and honor about God. I didn't come from something *other*; these mom characteristics are God characteristics. Some of us display these in our homes with our children; other ezers demonstrate these characteristics in classrooms, with little sisters, as mentors, or in any setting where a maternal nature gets activated. We need to own it, whether a baby came out of our bodies or not.

Like God, mothers protect. "Like a bear robbed of her cubs, I will attack them and rip them open; like a lion I will devour them—a wild animal will tear them apart" (Hosea 13:8).

That's how mama bears act: fiercely protective of the bodies and souls of their children. So does Jesus; He fights for us: body and soul. A mother's heart is an immeasurable and magnificent thing; it has an almost infinite capacity to be misunderstood, overlooked, underappreciated, sacrificed, and judged—by the people she loves most. For most women, it's worth it: fighting for, protecting, and serving. She doesn't know any different; it's imprinted in her from the Creator she emulates.

In the beginning of my work with orphaned and vulnerable children, I saw the mothers of the orphans we served as two dimensional. I often thought judgmentally, *Who could leave this little one behind? Who would ever abandon this angel?* But somewhere over the last twenty-five years, my heart changed. Some of those angels grew up to become mothers themselves, and the ones who never addressed their core wounds lived very hard lives and often repeated the patterns of their childhoods. That's when I learned that the moms whose choices I didn't understand were often grown-up girls with traumatic histories, who never received the healing relationships they needed to change their trajectories. They had needed protection so they could learn to protect others.

Like God, mothers remember their children. "Can a woman forget her nursing child and have no compassion on the son of her womb? Even these may forget, but I will not forget you" (Isaiah 49:15 NASB). Women have perpetual dashboards in our minds with dials for work, our people, and anything else we have going on. We know what the weather is, where the next game is, what each child's reading level is—and a thousand other details, *simultaneously*, about aging parents, best friends, work responsibilities, and still—we will not forget our children. Those windows are always open. While Todd can be engrossed where he is—and there's tremendous benefit to his focus—ezer-moms (with exceptions, of course) always have a window open for their children. And that's how God is. We are always on His mind.

Like God, mothers long to gather their children together. "Jerusalem, Jerusalem, you who kill the prophets and stone those sent to you, how often I have longed to gather your children together, as a hen gathers her chicks under her wings, and you were not willing" (Luke 13:34). This was my favorite part about the pandemic: all the kids were together at Camp Guckenberger. That's how God is. He likes it when we gather; it's been His plan since the beginning. He created His people to be in His place, so they can experience His presence and have His peace. It started that way in Genesis and will finish that way in Revelation. When we have those longings, moms, we are exercising that God-like nature in us.

Like God, mothers comfort. "As a mother comforts her child, so will I comfort you" (Isaiah 66:13). Right after we adopted our son Tyler, we took an already-scheduled family vacation to Colorado. It is no one's good idea to take a twelve-year-old who has just moved from another country and disrupt his adjustment with travel, but we forged on, knowing the rest of the household would be disappointed if we canceled. He tried many new things for the first time—hiking, fishing, and horseback riding—which were overstimulating and unknown to him.

One night, the family was playing Monopoly, yet another new experience for him. Tyler was trying to keep up, but the boys began laughing, and he thought his new brothers were making fun of him. The next minute, Tyler threw the board up in the air. I knew he was tired, so I ushered him, crying, away from the family and into his room to go to bed. I assumed he was exhausted and would fall asleep in minutes. I was shocked when, an hour later, one of my sons let me know he was still crying in bed.

I hurried into his room, at this point knowing his tears were no longer about Monopoly. They were the grieving, confused tears of a boy whose whole life had changed in a month. I just curled up in bed next to him and told him what I knew was true.

"We love you."

"I'm not going anywhere."

"You are safe."

Eventually, he fell asleep.

On the way home, I made everyone tell me their favorite part of vacation. One by one, they shared activities that had cost us money. Everyone was curious when it was Tyler's turn. Of all the new he had tried, which activity would be his favorite?

"That's easy," he said. "My favorite moment of vacation was when Mom told me how much she loved me."

Mama's comfort ... and we are just a dim reflection of God, who wants to hold us, to tell us what is true, and to remind us He won't leave.

Like God, mothers look for the lost. "Or what woman, having ten silver coins, if she loses one coin, does not light a lamp and sweep the house and seek diligently until she finds it? And when she has found it, she calls together her friends and neighbors, saying, 'Rejoice with me, for I have found the coin that I had lost.' Just so, I tell you, there is joy before the angels of God over one sinner who repents" (Luke 15:8–10 ESV).

This parable comes in a set of three: a lost coin, a lost sheep, and a lost son. All are metaphors for the One in pursuit of us. Mothers, have any of you ever longed for and loved someone who was lost? I have ... with a feeling inside like I won't stop, and I don't care how I find you or what condition I find you in. Those are God-feelings, God-reflections of the way He made us. It's beautiful to be on a search for those we love who are lost; it's a holy act. The more a woman lives out her soulful reflection of the Shepherd who once found her, the more beautiful she becomes. She has an inner beauty indicating her soul is on fire. It's alluring to see, not in a sexual sense, but in a can't-take-your-eyes-off-her way. A woman on a mission to love and seek the lost is attractive in a way hair dye, makeup, or surgery can't affect.

These characteristics—shielding, comforting, birthing, protecting, hovering—are God qualities, and they manifest in us ezers because we are of Him and from Him. We don't need to apologize for or minimize it. We don't need to say "I'm just being a mom" or let someone mock us for exercising who we were made to be.

These characteristics—shielding, comforting, birthing, protecting, hovering—are God qualities, and they manifest in us ezers because we are of Him and from Him.

We each offer something unique to reflect what God first gave *to* us. Nothing is an accident: where we were born, or our kids, or where we live, or our giftings, or our quirks. This is all part of a Great Plan, and our days were ordained before any of them came to be (Psalm 139:16). We came from Him, we reflect Him, we honor Him, we love Him, and we are pursued by Him. We live "for such a time as this" (Esther 4:14) because there is no other reason to live for any other time than now. The stakes are that high.

Let's make room for the women around us to use their unique gifts and respect and honor how God *created* them. They are protective and fierce. They are frontline and prayer warriors, in the trenches fighting for their families and friends. Let's be fully who we are, embracing our divine and maternal nature. The Church can't afford for us to hold back.

Questions to Consider

Which characteristic typically associated with moms have you experienced in God?

Who is always on your mind?

In what settings is it hardest for you to express yourself?

Journal

Which characteristics of yourself do you believe came from Him?

Chapter 15

What does being a warrior have to do with invitation?

Jesus was a bold inviter. He didn't care who was watching, and He went out of His way to include "all nations" (Isaiah 56:7). He modeled invitation and courage and revolutionary thinking. I often say the Bible can be summed up in two words: "Come" and "Go." He is an invitational God who invites us into a relationship, and He is a Great Commissioner, inviting us to go out and model the same. Either way, He invites. He wants to live life with us, to share in our days, the highs and the lows. He wants to be intimate with us, telling us words and giving us pictures only we are privy to. He wants to lead our meetings, be on vacation with us, and listen to our endless conversations. He wants to comfort us when we hurt and celebrate with us when we win. He wants us all, and all of Him He offers.

When someone is loved well by the people of God, they fall in love with the God of those people. This is how God designed it. In the New Testament, written in Greek, there are three words we translate as "love": friendship love, romantic love, and the kind of love Jesus had for us, which comes from the word *agape*. *Agape* has a big, long definition, but my favorite part is that agape love is compelled to act. Ezers look most like Jesus when compelled to act. But act on what? What can we do for others? How can we help?

I met two girls when they were eleven, twins living in a children's home in Mexico where we were serving. They spent a lot of weekends and holidays with my family before coming to our home full-time at age fifteen. This choice asked us to be present, and our presence—people wholly focused on their well-being—was a rare and beautiful gift they'd never had. In the following years as they assimilated into our home, our investment in their lives bore incredible fruit. Because we came for them

> unguarded (go ahead, reject me),
> undistracted (nothing is more important than you right now),
>   and
> without judgment (wherever you've been and whatever you are
>   thinking, I still want you).

Presence *matters*, and being fully present with them was part of the secret sauce God used in their healing. Today, they are adult women who have given us wonderful grandchildren, but I couldn't have imagined those storylines when we invited them into our family. When we open our hearts, arms, tables, and homes, we can get swept up into God's bigger story, which is more than we see in the moment of our *yes*.

Twenty years ago, while I was living in Mexico, a baby was dropped off at a nearby children's home. I kept an eye on her as she was growing up, and through the years she was on a program track destined for higher education. However, a few years ago she got pregnant, dropped out, and married one of the young men in the same program. This could feel like a "failure," but all of us are living a story still being told, and we can be confident that God never stops working.

That young woman's baby is now in elementary school, and this past summer, her husband was in a near-fatal motorcycle accident while riding to work. Her first call in the middle of the night was to a Back2Back staff member who had stayed present with them both since they'd left the program. The young man miraculously survived, but he has no memory of his life or most of his skills before the accident. He is having to relearn everything, including his name and how to eat; everything is new for him.

These are long stories, and this couple is changing even now as I write this. Amid this painful season, God is reintroducing Himself to them, and their need for Him is powerful. Through consistent care and discipleship, they are growing up and growing unified. Their hearts have been enlarged by suffering, and they are rapidly healing. God does this all the time. He heals more than just the body; He is using the staff woman to help heal their souls and relationship. I told her recently, "You are it. God's chosen on this earth to demonstrate His ridiculous mercy and care for us. Through your consistent pursuit of them for years, you demonstrated when it counted: *they belong*." We long in the deepest part of ourselves to belong.

We long in the deepest part of ourselves to belong.

Some stories in life go exactly the way we want ... they're amazing and we love telling them. But I am not afraid to say some stories don't go down the way we plan. We can ezer with all our hearts and it's still not enough. Or who we reach for doesn't reach back. Or we tucker ourselves out. Or someone else comes in and ruins what we built. It all happens. We can eventually give up if our Christian life seems like a lot of just trying harder and feeling worse.

Amid the stories we don't like and can't control, God doesn't give up on anyone. His promises are still good: to come to us, hear us, lift us up, execute true justice on our behalf, extend mercy toward us ... He is always looking for vessels in His pursuit of people. He invites us to invite others into the family. Relentlessly.

Ezers are known for reaching out and holding on. I've seen women never give up in stories the rest of us look at and assume are hopeless. I've seen ezers cross roads, picket lines, fences, and classrooms to build connections and extend invitations. There's something fierce about feminine strength. (My husband calls it the "velvet hammer." It comes down hard but somehow feels soft.) This is it: the invitation to engage that won't be refused.

For Jesus, hospitality was not a task but a way of life. He's who we are to model in our inviting, with an overflow of our gratitude for the love and welcome of God toward us. My life verse is "Because we loved you so much, we were delighted to share with you not only the gospel of God but our lives as well" (1 Thessalonians 2:8). Sharing our lives is critical ezer work; it's helping with long-term vision.

While we were raising our children in Mexico, our son's first word was *pásale*, meaning "come in" in Spanish, because he heard me saying it all day long. Someone would knock on the door, looking for something, someone, help, fellowship ... and the answer was yes, *pásale*. We welcome—family, strangers, neighbors, enemies— because God first welcomed us while we were still enemies and strangers. It's usually messy and inconvenient, and honestly, that's kind of the point.

"But God demonstrates his own love for us in this: While we were still sinners, Christ died for us" (Romans 5:8). He said *"pásale"* to us.

As an illustration of invitation, God used tables throughout Scripture. In Psalms, He talked about setting tables before our enemy. In Isaiah, the prophet described heaven as a table set for a wedding feast. In the Gospels, Jesus sat at tables with people no one approved of. In Revelation 3:20 John wrote, "Here I am! I stand at the door and knock. If anyone hears my voice and opens the door, I will come in and eat with that person, and they with me."

Tables were more than just places to eat; they demonstrated mutual trust. Sitting at the same table meant you shared a protected relationship. The people you ate with revealed something about who you were, showing to whom you belonged. When the Lord talks about dining with us, He is inviting us into an intimate relationship that is celebrated with a meal together.

In the Luke 7:36–50 story, Jesus was the dinner guest of Simon the Pharisee. Sharing a meal was important in the ancient world; who you did and didn't invite to your table was socially determined. Tables were one way of maintaining social structures, so everyone paid attention to everything. We know some people at the dinner were reclining at the table, a common way to eat for those who were wealthy or privileged. They would lean on their left arms, with their feet out behind them. Only a free citizen could recline; women, children, and slaves, if they were present, had to sit upright.

In the Middle East, dinner parties weren't held behind closed doors; the houses were open, with lots of coming and going. It was not unusual for those who weren't invited to hang out around the edges of the group, listening in on the discussions. Into this combination of people—invited guests and curious observers—came a sinful woman from the city. She didn't break into Simon's house, which we might assume given how we host dinner parties. She came up behind Jesus and began to weep, washing His feet with her tears and drying them with her hair. She took ointment and anointed His feet. In these actions, she embodied first-century hospitality.

Since the roads are dusty and people wore sandals, it was the host's job to wash the guests' feet (or see it done). It was also customary for the host to kiss the guest and possibly anoint them with oil. Because Simon neglected to do these things, he didn't fulfill his role as host. This uninvited guest, this woman, ezer, acted as the host as she washed Jesus' feet.

I recognize the feminine grit in this story. How many times have you had to make your way into a room you weren't invited to, take on a role usually left to a man, make a scene, and not care who was watching? This is classic ezer activity. And what does this warrioring/helping look like? Like a host, like initiation, like worship.

Sometimes Jesus is the host, but in this case, He was the guest. In most of the biblical stories, Jesus moved freely between the roles of host and guest. Usually, He was a guest in someone's home, but when He broke bread and offered it to others, He acted as a host. Throughout Jesus' ministry, we learn that at Jesus' table guests become hosts and hosts become guests; everyone has something to give and something to receive. And that's an important part of invitation: we all need what the other brings to the table. This is a ripe environment for two planks to prop up against each other, co-laboring.

Questions to Consider

Who has been invitational toward you?

When was a time that an invitation was noticeably lacking?

Are you more comfortable as host or guest?

Journal

Who do you sense God asking you to invite to your table?

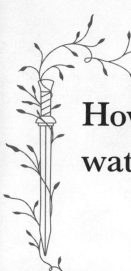

Chapter 16

How can ezers add more water to their beans?

In Spanish, when more people come for a meal than you plan, you say you'll "add more water to the beans." Meaning you'll use what you have, add what you need to stretch to meet the demand, and trust that God covers it. When we step into our God-given nature as inviters, we regularly find that God adds more water to the beans; He gives us what we need.

In the very act of inviting, we risk and make ourselves vulnerable. Jesus said, "Do not throw your pearls to pigs" (Matthew 7:6), painting a vivid word picture. He could've said, "Be careful you do not give something precious to someone who does not appreciate its beauty; they might trample on it." The space you hold—your heart, the calling you've heard, your stories, the beauty you possess—these are your pearls. When you offer them, it makes you vulnerable, but not weak. The very act of risking rejection makes the gift all the braver and the giver stronger.

I was taking some women through an exercise called Lectio Divina, Latin for "divine reading." It's an old practice that dates back to the monks hundreds of years ago. Many variations exist, but typically someone reads a passage of Scripture out loud several times, prompting you to listen for words or phrases that stand out, or they encourage you to see pictures God might be prophetically giving you.

I requested everyone to close their eyes and listen as I read from Isaiah 43 about God being with us, whether in the fire or high waters. I told them to imagine a canvas and to ask God to paint something, illustrating His Word. Then we prayed those images and words back to Jesus.

One woman was quiet, seeming not to participate, although I could see she was emotionally moved by the tears brimming in her eyes. I didn't draw attention to her, just prayed God would give her something she knew was from Him. Suddenly she said quietly, "I see a candy store, and everyone, all of you, are inside, picking what you want, sampling new treats, being delighted. But I am on the outside of the window, pressing my face to the glass, watching everyone enjoy their candy, while I am without."

What a privilege it was to say to her, "You are invited into that candy shop. Those good gifts, those treats, are for *you*. Sample what you want ... everything He has, He offers to you." Women came around her, laying hands on her, praying over her. They listened to her questions and stuck close.

In God's family, there is joy and celebration when the lost are found, the hungry are fed, the lonely are brought into relationship, and the homeless are given shelter. This is the charge of Isaiah 58.

> "Is not this the kind of fasting I have chosen:
> to loose the chains of injustice
>   and untie the cords of the yoke,
> to set the oppressed free
>   and break every yoke?
> Is it not to share your food with the hungry
>   and to provide the poor wanderer with shelter—
> when you see the naked, to clothe them,
>   and not to turn away from your own flesh and blood?
> Then your light will break forth like the dawn,
>   and your healing will quickly appear;

then your righteousness will go before you,
    and the glory of the LORD will be your rear guard.
Then you will call, and the LORD will answer;
    you will cry for help, and he will say: Here am I. (verses 6–9)

This is my testimony: while I try to do what God's asked of me, I am in over my head every time. I am never enough, and yet, I've found He's always there, answering my cries for help, being my portion. Seeing the needs of others requires a total reprioritizing and reordering of our lives. It's not just being with those who are easy, or whom I can benefit from being with. It's refusing to be selfish, self-absorbed, or self-serving, and instead, I will be inconvenienced, vulnerable, curious, and in relationship. I just can't do that consistently without crying out for help.

Invitation is a God-idea: Abraham welcomed the angels (Genesis 18:1–15), the widow at Zarephath provided food for Elijah (1 Kings 17:7–24), Lydia opened her home to the church (Acts 16:13–15), Rahab was rewarded because she protected Joshua's spies (Joshua 2; 6:17), Paul instructed elders to be hospitable (1 Timothy 3:2), the writer of Hebrews said to show hospitality to strangers (Hebrews 13:2), and Peter admonished we are to "show hospitality to one another without grumbling" (1 Peter 4:9 ESV). Jesus practiced hospitality without a home and generosity without a salary, and God talked about welcome from Genesis to Revelation.

"For I was hungry and you gave me food, I was thirsty and you gave me drink, I was a stranger and you welcomed me, I was naked and you clothed me, I was sick and you visited me, I was in prison and you came to me." Then the righteous will answer him, saying, "Lord, when did we see you hungry and feed you, or thirsty and give you drink? And when did we see you a stranger and welcome you, or naked and clothe you? And when did we see you sick or in prison and visit you?" And the King will answer them, "Truly, I say to you, as you did it to one of the least of these my brothers, you did it to me." (Matthew 25:35–40 ESV)

Jesus is not saying, "If you do these things, you'll be saved." Salvation is not based on works. He is showing us acts of welcome to *condition us* into not only believing in the King but being kingdom-minded people.

He is showing us acts of welcome to *condition us* into not only believing in the King but being kingdom-minded people.

An executive pastor was giving me a tour of his church's campus. As we entered the children's area, I couldn't help but notice it was more like a park—bigger than you would typically see at a church or even a school.

"What's the deal with the playground?" I asked, wondering if a donor had paid for it.

"Our pastor's wife, an adoptive parent, went to the county social services and asked what we could do as a church to serve them. She knew the county was understaffed and overpopulated with vulnerable children. They told her if we wanted to do something to address supervised visits, that would be amazing. When birth parents had visitation with their children in foster care, they were shown to a small conference room with a cardboard box full of tired toys. No one wanted to be there, least of all the children."

His eyes lit up; this story was part of their church lore. "We just needed to provide a shelter and accessible bathrooms; the rest we could make up as we pleased. We dreamt about a place where children would want to come, and parents would feel proud to bring them. Now, we have weekly volunteers who staff the playground. They talk to nervous foster parents while birth-parent visitation is happening and pray with birth parents when foster families drive away. It's allowed us to minister to the whole spectrum of families, just through this playground." That is making room. What happens in that space is up to God.

In Exodus 25, Moses recorded what God said in verse 8, "Then have them make a sanctuary for me, and I will dwell among them." God was telling Moses if he would make room for Him, He would fill the space. We can make room for God in our relationships, in our decisions, in our questions, in our dreams, in everything, and God will fill the space. The invitation comes in many forms. Maybe He's asking me to invite someone to my table, or maybe into my family. I just know anytime I use what's at my disposal to include someone, it's ezer-like.

Every evening in our home, we share our "happy's and crappy's" at dinner. It keeps us empathetic to each other's stories and gives us a reason to celebrate one another. This kind of intentional conversation allows us to appreciate the diversity in our relationships. We can share with people twice or half our age, the same or wildly different. I am always asking myself, *Am I being proximate to cultures, races, ages, and others different from me?* If I only come for or invite my "own" people, I am not much of an ezer. I could be accused of building my own kingdom instead of His. God often asks us to do what isn't familiar, not for the shock of it, although it can be shocking, but because His way is so *other*. The result is a colony of heaven, demonstrating we are a people who belong to God.

In Acts 16, Paul planted a church in Philippi, a colony of Rome. When you were in Philippi, it was as if you were in Rome. The people's citizenship was Roman, and so was their culture, language, and money. So when Paul later wrote to them in Philippians 3:20, "Our citizenship is in heaven," he was saying, "We are now a colony too." When people are around us, they should feel as if they are in a colony of heaven. Our marriages, neighborhoods, and workplaces should bring heaven to earth. Our churches today should especially put this on display. The church isn't just a place we attend; it's a place we belong, and Sundays are pep rallies to encourage us to keep going back out there to colonize heaven. All Christ followers have this calling, but it takes courage, humility, and copious amounts of love to get there. It is a fight fit for a warrior.

In God's colony, the rules of social class, race, ethnicity, ability, family, gender, and culture are upside down. He honors us when we join in the radical work of the kingdom, looking beyond what we are taught to see and treat people as they were created. If I want to be an effective helper-ezer, I need to understand what it looks like to make room for others—inviting people into the kingdom of God, where they can offer their gifts, experience His grace and mercy, be generous, take a risk, and dream.

We might be tempted to think the highest level of ezering includes best-in-class examples in their field, but elite ezers are room makers. Ezers are inviters because Jesus was, and opening space and pulling people in is some of the best warrioring we will ever do.

Questions to Consider

When have you cried out to Jesus for help in your weakness?

What are some biblical examples of invitation?

Who has purposely included you?

Journal

What is your comfort level with people who are different from you?

Chapter 17

What happens when we weaponize our charge to ezer?

Some details in the following story have been changed to obscure the identities of those involved, but the truth of the testimony remains.

Unhealthy ezers damage those around them.

I have a friend who provides me with a professional service. We initially met through work but over time have developed a sincere friendship. It's what makes what happened next so painful for me to confess.

Out of the blue, a woman offered me an amazing, too-good-to-be-true break on this same service, and I leaped at the opportunity. This was going to be amazing. The one caveat was I would need to let go of my friend's services and instead employ this new shiny apple. I hesitated slightly but then bit.

It became evident I had made a mistake when promises were broken and the big "break" meant me spending money I didn't anticipate. When confronted, this powerful, gifted, selfish woman ghosted me; I felt used.

We finished the contract, but I only interacted with her staff. I never talked to her in person again, so we never had closure, and she never apologized. I wanted to be mad at her, but the truth was, I was mad at myself. I give her credit for being an incredible businesswoman who was willing to do whatever was needed to achieve her goals, but I became the collateral damage. I had encountered an unhealthy ezer who probably *wanted* to do what she had promised but, in the end, never took responsibility for her actions.

As the opportunity fell apart, it was made even worse as I grieved the hurt my decision caused my friend. I now faced a few choices:

> Stick with the broken arrangement and deny I made a mistake.
> Discontinue her services, but (in shame) never circle back with my friend.
> Return to my friend and ask forgiveness, learn a hard lesson, and move on.

I knew the first two choices would mean adding my unhealthiness to hers, and that's never a good idea. Desiring to be a healthy ezer necessitated admitting to my own personal ambition and greed. I wasn't sure whether my friend would accept my apology, but I called and asked him to forgive me. I confessed how distracted I had been by a path of least resistance, and I apologized for how quickly I had dismissed our history. I am pleased to report I am back in his professional and personal good graces, but not without the work of confession it required.

I was telling myself an unhealthy story *about* myself, one where I was successful and important rather than principled and loyal. The Bible study resource *Gospel Transformation* says:

> Stories define how we think, how we behave, how we feel about others and about ourselves ... we have a fantasy world filled with stories where we are more successful, better-known, more loved, admired, and desired, more in control, in better health, and living in peace and comfort. Thus viewed in this light, and considering the Gospel as a story, our lives are a conflict of stories—one trying to rule the other.
>
> If we belong to Jesus, God has given us a new image, status, and reputation. God has made us right. This is an essential part of

the Gospel story. If we forget this part, we start inventing our own stories to improve our reputation and our image before others.[25]

Every time I prefer my version of a story to the gospel, I act unhealthy and am in no position to help anyone. I needed God to heal my heart and my appetite for sin. Jeremiah 2:13 says it like this: "My people have committed two sins: They have forsaken me, the spring of living water, and have dug their own cisterns, broken cisterns that cannot hold water."

An accountability partner and I refer to the difference between drinking "dirty water" and "clean water." When I am in the Word, drinking the spring of Living Water, I can tell when something is too good to be true. When I get used to consuming dirty water, I lose my ability to discern, or worse, I develop a taste for it. It's critical to stay healthy or we spend our lives cleaning up the consequences of poor choices.

Have you ever heard of "Sheilaism"? Its origin is from some research done in the 1980s, when Robert Bellah, the author of *Habits of the Heart*, interviewed a woman named Sheila Larson on her religious habits and patterns. She answered, "I believe in God.... My faith has carried me a long way. It's Sheilaism. Just my own little voice."[26] Today, the term *Sheilaism* means someone who has incorporated various faith practices and combined them with their own understanding and intuition, their own religion of one. We live in a culture that is wildly validating to people who have their own concoction of beliefs. And Sheilaism is perhaps our most popular and active faith in the US. We see it on media, in our modern music anthems, and reinforced on social media. It sounds like, "Listen to yourself." "Trust yourself." "Be your own boss." "Own your truth." "You do you." It is the opposite message of "Deny yourself, pick up your cross, and follow Me" (see Matthew 16:24).

Biblically, that kind of inward-focused faith leads to death.

How do we stay emotionally healthy? How do we not take the ezer charge and run people over with it? We follow biblical text. The same text that empowers us will guide us in using that power. God invites us into His rhythm, and it starts with listening and resting, not charging and leading and fighting. Step one in being a powerful, healthy ezer is to be still. Stillness is an act of self-care. Jesus modeled that for us when He went to the mountain to pray (Luke 6:12). God directed fiery Elijah to wait for the still, small voice (1 Kings 19:11–12), and David said over and again in Psalms how important stillness was to his spiritual posture. "My heart is not proud, LORD, my eyes are not haughty; I do not concern myself with great matters or things too wonderful for me. But I have calmed and quieted myself, I am like a weaned child with its mother; like a weaned child I am content" (Psalm 131:1–2).

God invites us into His rhythm, and it starts with listening and resting, not charging and leading and fighting.

I have never liked it when someone told me to rest (not as a child, not in a sports setting, not as we built our family and ministry), so I am sensitive about writing something that doesn't shame but fosters curiosity about what a rhythm of rest could look like. For rest to be effective, it has to be more than a Sabbath, more than a weekly strategy or even a yearly one. It's a daily decision to rest. It's understanding that what happens in my mind is as important as what happens with my body. I can stop and sit in a chair, technically *resting*, but still be working, wound up in ideas or anxiety that keeps my engine running. I can also go outside and exercise, be in motion (seemingly the opposite of rest), and experience the break I need.

I can tell when I start to get imbalanced because I struggle in a couple of areas. One is not allowing for transition time in my day. Instead of letting my heart and mind settle from what I just did and prepare for what I am about to do, I use transition time for more work, multitasking in the car, etc. This results in an anxious pace, where I've left little time to talk or listen to God and I go blindly into whatever I have planned next. I find myself chronically late, and if something unexpected comes up, I have no margin to manage it. A day like that and I leave a trail of consequences in my wake.

Another sign I am operating in an unhealthy state is when I can't put down my mental load: the constant lists of who I am thinking or worrying about and the tasks I need to accomplish. What a gift when I put that down, and yet, without intentional rest, I can carry it day after day and grow weary from its weight. Then I feel stretched, wearisome, and overwhelmed and still try to do my ezer-like helping, but from a deficit. Rest is realizing I can stop *thinking* so much and for a moment— let it go. I am not "letting it go" into the ethos, as if I no longer care; I am placing it in the hands of the One who can carry it lightly.

The reality of how I handle these two strategies in my day—zero transitions and a heavy mental load—speaks to my view of God. The natural drift of my heart is in the direction of self-reliance, so I need to create a lifestyle that steers my heart toward what the Lord values (connection) rather than what the world seeks (ambition). When other things count, I take my eyes off the gospel. I spend all my energy protecting the stories or outcomes that I think will bring me joy, and the focus that takes does not leave me much to love or help others. When I rest, I reset, remember where my GPS is set, and stop compelling and scheming outcomes that aren't mine to determine.

The only thing that matters is that we believe the gospel and love others.

Rest was always God's idea. God started His story, authored as He willed, by including the detail of rest in the creation story: after six days of work, there was a day of rest. We have Sabbath to imitate that pattern. But we are more hurried, tired, and disconnected than ever before in this country. We need rest. The average American picks up their phone eighty times a day. Despite knowing social media has strong ties to anxiety and depression, when we sit down to unwind, we pick up our phones. Why was Calm the app of the year? Because we were created (and long) for it. Rest restores in a way no technology, food, or bad habit can. We were not created to carry all the information and burdens our pocket computers spew at us all day.

> Six days you shall do your work, but on the seventh day you shall rest; that your ox and your donkey may have rest, and the son of your servant woman, and the sojourners, may be refreshed. (Exodus 23:12 ESV)

I appreciate the insight offered by Bible teacher Lois Tverberg on this verse:

> Who is supposed to be refreshed when the people of Israel observe the Sabbath? It's the *animals* and the *slaves* and the *sojourners*....
>
> In order to understand [this command], you need to think *communally.... As a community you shall rest....* No way that animals and slaves could observe the Sabbath without the permission of their owners. If a landowner decided that it was a good day for plowing, his slaves and animals had little choice but to obey him. Sojourners were just as powerless, working as migrant laborers and hired help.[27]

God wants each one of us to experience a rhythm of weekly rest and worship. But according to this verse, the refreshment of the Sabbath was intended for the *ones who could not rest* without the permission of others. The goal of the Sabbath was not religiosity, but restoration. God wanted all His creation to be allowed a chance to relax and breathe and return to its original Eden-like state.

While an unhealthy ezer is selfish, rushes, and creates dire consequences for herself and the community around her, a healthy ezer keeps room in her life for healthy practices, to the benefit of everyone around her.

Questions to Consider

As an ezer, how does your relationship with work and rest impact others?

What are some signs you may be unhealthy?

When are you tempted to concoct your own beliefs?

Journal

How do you rest?

Chapter 18

So ... when *can* a warrior rest?

Speaking at a retreat out of town, I learned that before my time to share, the organizers had slotted in a Christian clown. I wasn't thrilled to follow a Christian clown. *What did that even mean?* Knowing nothing about this man or his program, my judgmentalism kicked in, my all-too familiar sin pattern when I am tired.

When the evening was over, I headed to the parking garage for the trip home. I was startled when a voice from behind me called my name.

"Beth, hey, wait up. I wanted to meet you before you left. My name is Steve; I was the clown tonight," he said, then laughed. "You probably don't recognize me without my makeup."

I smiled, and we exchanged a few pleasantries.

He continued, "We are both headed down the same highway tonight. I pastor a church in your community. You might not have heard of us; we aren't very big ..." Looking me in the eye, his voice trailed off and he hesitated so long, I was uncertain he would continue. "... I learned of your ministry through a friend, and although we couldn't financially contribute, we still wanted to serve you. I called your office and asked for the names of your children, so we could pray for them."

I looked at him, a little shocked.

"The person who answered told me about your four youngest children, so I've had Emma, Evan, Josh, and Aidan on my prayer list and as a part of our Saturday morning intercession for the last five years. It's so good to finally meet you. Tell me, how are they doing?"

I didn't have words. I was convicted, inspired, ashamed, and blessed. I tried to speak but was too choked up to get the words out. I was embarrassed and knew I had thought an hour or two before that, as the preacher and not the clown, *I* was the more spiritual one of the two of us. But here I stood, realizing just the opposite was true. While I judged, he prayed.

Finally, I mumbled my heartfelt thanks and climbed into my car. I put my head on my steering wheel and told the Lord I was the kind of tired that a nap doesn't fix, and that fatigue leaves me at my spiritual worst. *Convict me!* I prayed because I needed conviction, but I also needed rest. Rest, so I could reconnect with the heart of the Father and align my thinking and my heart with His. It was like I was rushing along a city sidewalk and saw a $20 bill lying on the ground. Instead of taking a moment to pick it up, either because I was too tired to bend down, too much in a hurry to stop, or because I somehow thought I didn't need it, I'd been hurrying through life, missing out on moments where God had good gifts for me—necessary gifts. I wanted to stop. I wanted what He was littering the sidewalks of my life with, and I knew in some way, this clown was one of them.

When people ask me, "How do you balance it all?" I cringe. I *don't* balance it all. If my house looks good, then I probably haven't showered. If my hair looks great, don't look at my bathroom. If I'm killing it at work, I've ignored my children. If you see me at the zoo on Instagram, then I've put off my work. It's impossible to have the perfect body, house, marriage, work, children, social life, garden … the list goes on. How do I determine, amid those demands, where to bring my ezer? *Who do I help? When? How?* And if I am focused on my own body, house, marriage, work, children, social life, garden, etc., when do I have time to look up and see the needs of others?

I have a time-management system that ensures I spend my days with people I feel both called to and am uniquely designed for. My husband and I have a financial system that gives us margin and prevents financial stress. However, it's only in this recent season of my life that I have given *any* consideration to managing my energy output. In the past, I thoughtlessly gave away my energy throughout the day to whoever asked for it, as fast as I could. That left me exhausted in the evening and dangerously low on energy for my family or whatever came up in the last part of my day. I now think about my day in advance and consider what certain conversations and activities will cost me, and how I can find time to refill for what I anticipate still needing. It takes more intentionality and discipline than I am good at, and so I confess to doing it better some days than others.

Most of life is a what Bible translator and author Eugene Peterson calls a "long obedience" (marriage, parenting, work, neighboring ... the repetitive work of showing up to do the right thing over and over again, resulting in a form of holiness). As a finite being, I need to pray for the sensitivity to only carry what He is asking of me. There isn't room in my day or in my mind for a mental load greater than my capacity, and the result of trying to overachieve is burnout or, worse yet, failure.

Consider the difference between relief and restoration. One is reactive and the other is proactive. Relief is give-me-a-break-right-now and I can reach for things that feel good but aren't satisfying. I am looking for a distraction, something to not make me feel what I am feeling. The more I choose to pick up my phone, turn on the TV, eat, drink, shop, whatever, the less present I am to the needs of my heart, to the thoughts I need to take captive, to the disappointment I don't want to face. It's a short-term rest with long-term consequences.

A much better choice is a regular pattern of retreat and restoration, which refills for reengagement, breeds creativity, and feeds our sense of spiritual adventure. It gives us the chance to reload for future battles and serves to remind us Who and why we are warrioring. It's ultimately a chance to unclench and breathe. To let go of expectations and just be. I'm not responsible for people, crises, or trauma; God is. I can put it down; it's too hard to fight while carrying what I was never intended to. I am His vessel; He is the Commander. My soul is permeable. Don't ask me how I know this. I just sense that what comes at me should be able to flow in and out and not accumulate like a swimming pool with a filling deep end. There's only so much it can hold, and retreat gives me a chance to drain it and allow God to be infinite and me to just be ... human.

Relief releases intense pressure. If that's all you can get, take it, but don't settle for it. What's needed, what we crave, is restoration. It's encoded into us, this desire for renewal and rebirth. There are moments when we get backed into an emotional corner and just need it to all *stop*. In this instance, we are at risk of seeking relief with an escape, which leads to fantasies of quitting. According to the Environmental Protection Agency, Americans on average will spend approximately 90 percent of their life indoors,[28] which is a problem since nature is one avenue God gives us to restore. Deep restoration is experienced in nature, in prayer, in repose, and in relationships—take your pick, but pick something. Otherwise, our minds are somewhere between frantic and fried, and we try to learn something new, problem-solve, and think creatively on only a fraction of the capacity God has given us. I confess: I've been in a hurry and multitasking all my life ... I thought I was making up time. Maybe I've been throwing it away.

The Hebrew word for "desert" is *midbar*, which also means "the place of the Word." God regularly led His people into the desert (or "wilderness") so they would come to depend on Him, to hear from Him. As I feel the heat of the desert, I can complain, *Why am I here? It's too much, Lord*—when it's possible God led me there to talk to me. "But now I am going to woo her—I will bring her out to the desert and I will speak to her heart" (Hosea 2:14 CJB). Above what I do for Him, or where I go, He cares most about my heart. And if He brings me to the desert, it's with the romantic passion of a lover who wants to get away with me. He's not bringing me there for reprimand or to sit on the time-out chair. He wants to meet me face to face, like He did with Moses (Exodus 33), and remind me of our love story.

Jesus would say something in Matthew that would be shocking to His audience only because they were familiar with the following two passages:

> "This is what the LORD says: 'Stand at the crossroads and look;
> ask for the ancient paths, ask where the good way is, and walk
> in it, and you will find rest for your souls'" (Jeremiah 6:16).

> "My presence will go with you, and I will give you rest" (Exodus
> 33:14).

So when Jesus talked about rest in Matthew 11:28–30, "Come to me, all you who are weary and burdened, and I will give you rest. Take my yoke upon you and learn from me, for I am gentle and humble in heart, and you will find rest for your souls," *He was claiming to be the path to God.*

He was saying rest doesn't come from a nap or a break; it comes when we stay within His will.

Rest realigns; it recommits us to a life we feel purpose in. Have you ever thought, *How did I get here? When did this happen?* Sabbath rest is designed to be a check-in: *Did something get out of sync and is on pause? Can I course correct?* I had to get over the idea that rest is not a reward; it simultaneously allows for vulnerability and comfort. And it comes in all kinds of forms. I can rest while driving my convertible: there's something about the music and the wind that allows me to breathe. I can rest while being intimate with my husband: the total focus and release of the day melting into pleasure. I can rest while trying a delicious meal: the flavors satisfying my hunger. I can see something in nature that is beautiful, and my soul sighs. There's a mysterious connection between rest, beauty, and pleasure; understanding what gives your soul a break will lead to more than a day off or an extra hour of sleep.

Understanding what gives your soul a break will lead to more than a day off or an extra hour of sleep.

John 10:10 promises we were intended to live life to the full, with abundance. I can sometimes confuse abundance as "more," when it instead refers to the richness I forgo for a load not mine to carry. English evangelist Graham Cooke says that "rest is a weapon." What is it a weapon against? The attack of the enemy. Rest isn't a sign of weakness; it's a nod to someone's strength.

I did some original language study for *rest*. According to early translations from Hebrew to Greek, the word *hesuchazo* means "to rest, to be quiet, to be still." It's found in the Septuagint, and while those translators aren't considered infallible, their scholarship does offer insight. It's found in a passage familiar to me. "If you do well, will not your countenance be lifted up? And if you do not do well [Septuagint reads 'be still,' *hesuchazo*, a command in the aorist imperative to be still or silent], sin is crouching at the door; and its desire is for you, but you must master it" (Genesis 4:7 NASB).

My sin at the door may be different from your sin at your door. But what we have in common is, without rest, we are more at risk of sin overcoming us. I went to a professional soccer game this past week, and I could tell one player didn't want to come off the field when his coach pulled him out of the game, even though he was getting noticeably slower. After some rest, however, he burst back onto the field. I am no different: without stopping, I get weaker. Rest gives me the strength to continue.

Mark Buchanan wrote in *The Rest of God*:

> To refuse Sabbath is in effect to spurn the gift of freedom....
>
> Rest, it turns out, is a condition of liberty....
>
> Sabbath is a refusal to go back to Egypt....
>
> It was an exercise to teach the Israelites, not just obedience, but dependency.... [Sabbath] is about trust ... letting go, for one day out of seven, all those parts of our identities and abilities in which we are constantly tempted to find our security and discovering afresh that we are his children and that he is our Father and shield and defender.[29]

I sometimes hold on to more than I was designed for ... stuck in the day, feeling hopeless, thinking it's up to me, wanting to pretend something is better than it is, wanting to control what I don't like or didn't have planned, feeling the pressure of an over-full schedule or the conviction of an unconfessed sin or the fear of the future.

I've been whispering to myself lately, *You are not a machine*, because I have expectations of myself similar to those of my laptop, coffee maker, or water heater. I expect them to always work on demand. I can expect myself to perform when sometimes I feel burdened by all I am carrying, and the best way I can go forward is to reboot. Most of those machines, if they are malfunctioning, need to be turned off for a minute and then turned back on. I am no different. Sometimes, I just need to turn it all off for a moment.

For ezer, to help means I have enough for what *I* need plus so much that I can lend some to you. It's not serving from my deficit, or sacrificing myself on a sanctimonious altar ... I want my stores full and my resources ready to be deployed. I want to fight at full capacity. What do I need to do to get there? Listen to my body and soul. Pay attention to my heart. Renew my vision for what's ahead. We can't out-dream, out-vision, or out-hope God. I am determined to ask Him for more than I currently experience and trust it will keep me in the fight and prevent any fantasies of quitting and any lies about "it" not being worth my effort.

Questions to Consider

What is the difference between balance and imbalance in your life?

What brings you restoration?

Describe a season in your life that you spent in the desert. How did God meet you there?

Journal

What expectations do you place on yourself that you sense God isn't asking of you?

Chapter 19

Would you rather be a princess or a heroine?

I am so over the "God's princess" message. I know I am the daughter of the King, but what if we talked to this next generation of girls about being God's *heroine* instead?

During an informal survey I conducted online, I asked women to name their favorite heroines. There were so many entries about mothers and sisters, tales of their sacrifices and consistency. Reading their stories of resilience and courage made me want to be in *their* camp. These real-life women exhibit substance and grit and willpower, and those of us who have benefited from these qualities are quick to give credit to them. These women engage fully with their callings and live with adventure and intimacy with God.

I also heard names like Amelia Earhart, Rosa Parks, Mother Teresa, and Joan of Arc ... Clara Barton, Esther the Queen, Corrie ten Boom, Harriet Tubman, Elisabeth Elliot ... and the list goes on. What these women have in common are qualities we aspire to; they stood up for who and what they believed in. They had faithful lives and accepted challenging assignments.

People tend to admire a princess for her appearance, while a heroine is remembered for her actions. When we emphasize the more traditional option of being a princess, we risk the implication of focusing on one's *outer* beauty. Heroines are beautiful too, but typically for more than their clothes or hairstyles; heroines have notable *inner* beauty and strength. This isn't to say that beauty is bad. God made beauty, and He made it to delight us. Beauty is most evident when we feel alive, but somehow, we frequently reduce it to two-dimensional images based on ideals I am not sure I ever agreed to.

A heroine may be defined as "a woman admired or idealized for her courage, outstanding achievements, or noble qualities." Being a heroine may mean living, what is to you, an extraordinary life, not fulfilling someone else's ideas of who you should be, but creating a life based on what you sense God has deposited into your soul. He has a heart for the whole world; what portion has He placed in you? He has all the gifts, in full measure, so what gifts has He consigned to you? The expression of those gifts, on behalf of who you are called to, is the act of a heroine.

My favorite heroines see their every day as an opportunity to build another kingdom, to feed those hungry for substance over "stuff." They are also highly invitational, make space for others to join them on their mission, and are cooperative and community driven. They don't engage in the competition of princesses who have reduced beauty to scores, which today can look comparable to "likes" on social media posts and the ranking of someone's body on a scale of 1 to 10.

This is real to me as a woman, but even more so when I think about my daughters. I want to spend less time filtering what the world teaches them and more time captivating them with a greater truth. I can't protect them from the messages they absorb through media and peers, but I can purpose to tell them about their grandmothers and the Corrie ten Booms. I can remark as much about their attributes as I do their cute outfits. And I can be curious about what their mission is.

I spend a lot of time with young women who are paralyzed with not knowing what to do next. They are reaching out for an unknown future with an elusive mission that may not be what they thought for their lives or prepared for in college. Meanwhile, as they try and fail, or pivot or change their minds, it's all documented in such a spectacularly public way; they have the added pressure of wondering what everyone thinks about it. We have fed so many messages to them about fulfilling and realizing their dreams that when their first steps don't seem reportable, they assume they're on the wrong path. They spin their wheels wondering "Is this it?" as they pass by opportunities, people, work, and stories.

Heroines care more about *who* they are than what they *do*. The adventure, calling, and opportunities find them. Heroines have their eyes and hands open, trusting, believing, hoping, and dreaming of what they can co-create with their Creator. Here's to a new generation of women more prone to action than posing.

Here's to a new generation of women more prone to action than posing.

I couldn't put my finger on it at first. Why were social media posts of the women's march bothering me? I am a huge fan of women finding their voice and using it. I am often the only woman in rooms I go into, and I speak on Sundays in church settings, unafraid of theology that people used to say I shouldn't teach. I have mentored women from many countries, been the only female on national boards, and raised a half dozen daughters. I am a leader in a nonprofit. I *am* totally and completely pro-woman.

And yet ... watching the social media of women marching, I found myself simultaneously curious and frustrated. I wanted to ask the young women: Could you use a Saturday morning and the money it cost to travel more effectively? Would Jesus prefer you spend the time loving a woman rather than making signs and marching for her? For all the energy we spend in defense of women, what if we spent the same amount of time creating opportunities for, listening to, and investing in the lives of women around the world?

But to all women: words without actions create nothing more than entertainment. History has always been made by substantial women of action, not by the person with the most re-tweets or even the loudest voice. History has most often been made by women who used no words at all. We have a long line of heroines from whom to draw inspiration. They served in barrios, ran for office, and rose in the ranks; they studied and exceeded standards in the classroom and the courtroom.

These women made history. I am deciding to follow *their* example and try to be loving, excellent, and brave where I live and serve. Words may or may not be needed, but my prayer is my actions will speak louder than any slogan I could chant. It doesn't matter what policies we end up adopting; what we accomplish won't be effective in changing the world unless we love. Jesus tells us this.

Love comes from the heart, the alive-hopeful heart. The kind of heart that isn't discouraged, sees possibility, and doesn't just stick to her own kind. When I see one-sided conversations happening, I grow concerned that at some point people stopped listening. Yes, heroines pick battles they aren't sure they will win, and help those who may be hurting, but what if they also listen to people who sound wildly different from them? Heroines embark on uncertain adventures: not knowing where they'll lead, what it will cost them, or how they'll look to others in the process. They run to the front line and charge into the frontier, figuring it out as they go. They are students first, humble always, and brave in spades. They don't need to strive or prove anything, crediting their success to God. This kind of heroine is a beautiful woman, alive in her glory, and confident in her center that God says she is enough.

Consider Harriet Beecher Stowe, the seventh of twelve children of Lyman Beecher, a Congregationalist minister, revivalist, and reformer. She grew up to write *Uncle Tom's Cabin*, which highlighted the harsh conditions faced by African slaves. Her book had a powerful effect on the culture, stirring the controversy over slavery and leading many to see it as evil. Even one of her harshest critics acknowledged that it was "perhaps the most influential novel ever published, a verbal earthquake, an ink and paper tidal wave."[30] When she visited the White House, President Abraham Lincoln famously said to her, "So you're the little woman who wrote the book that started this great war."[31] She was a heroine.

We live in a world desperate to see our faith in action. If we want to work on behalf of the poor, we need to love a real person in poverty. If we want to be pro-life, we need to invite pregnant minors to our tables. If we say our hearts are breaking over the situation in the Middle East, with whom, where, when, and how are we engaged in helpful efforts beyond talking about them? If we say we are for women, then let's roll up our sleeves and get involved in the lives of women who are silenced, at risk, or vulnerable. Then our pictures won't be of women holding signs; they will be of women serving those whom Jesus loves through us.

How do we know Jesus loved women? He didn't have to say it; He lived it. He invited them to learn alongside everyone else. He trusted them with responsibilities. He gave them seats of honor. He spoke directly to them, listened intently to them, healed them, and commissioned them. His *actions* proved His conviction, and any movement that focuses more on how we act than how we look is a win for women.

Today, when the Church acts as Jesus did, we are graceful toward and empowering of women, making space for them in every sphere. He elevated women and set them on mission, and we should follow His example. Living as a heroine is wildly more compelling than aspiring to perfect princess outfits and camera poses. If someone is born with royal blood, they should use it to fight for people. Let's admire those women for their actions and not their clothes. Let's remember the biblical examples of women who used their resources and their gifts to advance the kingdom. There is power in this legacy, and it's ours for the taking.

Church, we should be leading in the treatment of women, not lagging. We are called to remember and celebrate our rich history of powerful women, and we are called to flip the script, just as Jesus did. Instead of following culture, let's influence it. May we raise up a new generation of women who see this message imprinted on the lives of those around them: *You have great worth.*

Questions to Consider

Who is an example of a heroine in your life?

What does supporting women look like to you?

Do you think faith communities are leading or lagging in the treatment of women? How can your community change?

Journal

What makes you feel like a heroine?

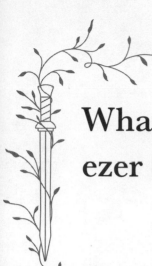

Chapter 20

What is a secure ezer capable of?

My sister-in-law was born and raised in Montana, and we laugh at our dissimilar lives. I can get around a foreign city; she can get around a ranch. In my work, I'm surrounded by children; in her work, she's surrounded by animals. I'm content with my gas fireplace; she's happiest around a campfire.

She's spent most of her adult life raising sheep and told me about an unusual phenomenon called "bum lambs" or "bummer lambs." When a ewe rejects her offspring, the shepherd or rancher brings it into the house, bottle-feeds it, and keeps it warm; otherwise, it won't survive. By holding it near a human heart, the lamb can hear a heartbeat, something critical to its early survival. When strong enough, it's returned to the flock.

From then on, when the shepherd or rancher comes out in the morning with feed, they call to the sheep and the first ones to come running are the bummer lambs, who by now have integrated into the flock. They *know* that voice, having learned it in their rejection when they were held close to the heart. It's a special relationship forged in tragedy.

In every way that counts, we were bummer lambs:

> rejected by the world,
> brought into His House, (where we)

experience God's heartbeat.

We learn His voice and

feel His supernatural compassion.

He soothes us.

When He says our name,

we know it's Him who saves us and who cares.

Both Drs. Dan Siegel and Curt Thompson have written about the human needs to be seen and soothed and to feel safe and secure. Those real needs we have can be met by God and then expressed through our most significant relationships. God can use others to soothe us, and He can also use us to help others feel safe. By extension, when an ezer is seen, soothed, safe, and secure, her potential to impact the world is exponential.

Last week during worship, I had a prophetic word for the person sitting next to me. (If this isn't in your faith tradition, I understand. It wasn't in mine for a very long time.) I describe prophecy as a thought that feels impressed upon my mind, something I don't feel I authored, and that is in alignment with what I understand the Scriptures to teach. The word was simple, "God sees you as a matriarch, a lineage starter." God saw the woman next to me and was saying, "I am doing something in you." I obediently witnessed it and expressed this encouragement to her.

God's been seeing and extending Himself toward us since the Garden. He reached out with compassion to a person (Noah), then a family (Abraham), then a nation (Moses), and then to the whole world (Jesus). He reached out to widows (Ruth) and orphans (Esther), strangers, sinners; in every story, in every corner, He is a reacher-outer.

The exchange we have with God over our rejections or broader hurts is one of the most precious we'll have on this side of eternity. He cares about our lament: a grieving of something that both mattered and shouldn't have happened. Almost

70 percent of the Psalms are considered laments. He does His best soothing when we come to Him with our questions and pain. It's not weakness, ezer, to admit confusion or hurt; it's strength to know where to go. Jesus doesn't want to just be who we read about in our quiet times or sing about in the car. He doesn't want to be our political affiliation or our country-club membership. Jesus wants to be our very essence, who we are desperate for. Then He can soothe us and make an unsafe world feel secure.

God wants to have a ministry of presence with us. Isaiah 49:13 says, "For the LORD comforts his people and will have compassion on his afflicted ones." We look like Him when we *see* others and are present with them. This is true with our friends, with the lost, with our Adam, and with our children. And the more intimate the relationship, the more potential we have to minister with our presence or to damage with our words. It's so vulnerable to *be* with people, especially when they are hurting. How we honor their hearts and that vulnerability is some of the most precious ezer-help we will offer.

God saw the biblical character Ruth, who was both a widow and a foreigner in need of provision, and He led her to Boaz's field, where she gleaned from the corners. He caused Boaz to see her. "Boaz asked the overseer of his harvesters, 'Who does that young woman belong to?'" (Ruth 2:5).

In the same way, He sees us: when we aren't looking, when we most need to be seen, and when we are going about our business. He then prompts others to see us and express His heart toward us: *on His behalf.* I can get turned around on this if I am not careful, wanting credit for myself when it belongs to God, or falsely crediting a person when their act of generosity or kindness was authored by God. It's He who sees us. This is clear throughout Scripture. Consider the example of Hagar, where in Genesis 16:13 it says, "She gave this name to the LORD who spoke to her: 'You are the God who sees me,' for she said, 'I have now seen the One who sees me.'"

In the Boaz and Ruth story, we see God soothe Ruth (as He soothes us). Ruth 3:11 says, "And now, my daughter, don't be afraid. I will do for you all you ask. All the people of my town know that you are a woman of noble character." Boaz extended himself toward her in a compassionate response prompted by God.

Compassion means "to suffer with," the idea being that what you are experiencing, I am willing to feel with you. Christians should be able to have proximity to pain because we know what to do with it. While our natural tendency with pain is to run away from it, ignore it, minimize it, or numb it, our supernatural selves can draw near to comfort. We can be present to soothe others because we've been soothed first by God. What work could more important than that? What would I possibly have to do that would trump those holy assignments?

We can be present to soothe others because we've been soothed first by God.

Ruth has been seen, soothed, and now feels safe (as we can feel too ...). Ruth 3:13 says, "Stay here for the night, and in the morning if he wants to do his duty as your guardian-redeemer, good; let him redeem you. But if he is not willing, as surely as the LORD lives I will do it. Lie here until morning." God creates the ultimate "felt safety" by promising to do what He says He will, especially when the stakes are high. He is good, and to be trusted. Felt safety, as defined by the late Dr. Karyn Purvis, is when you arrange the environment and adjust your behavior so your "children can feel in a profound and basic way that they are truly safe in their home and with [you]." Until this happens, "trust can't develop, and healing and learning won't progress."[32] With God, we can heal and learn because He is trustworthy. With Him, we have felt safety. Even when the world isn't safe.

What God did next in the story of Ruth was stunning: He made Ruth and Naomi secure (as we are secure in Him too). The last chapter is a reversal of the tragedy of the first chapter. Instead of losing a son, Naomi gained a son. Boaz sought out the nearest kinsman-redeemer (protector of the family line in a patriarchal society) to Ruth, and offered for him to take Ruth's land, with the understanding that she would come with it. That kinsman didn't want the complication of Ruth's presence and future offspring also coming to his family, so he relinquished his right (and actually his responsibility) to the next nearest kinsman: Boaz. The kinsman-redeemer should protect the persons, property, and prosperity of the family. Boaz *wanted* this responsibility!

> Then Boaz announced to the elders and all the people, "Today you are witnesses that I have bought from Naomi all the property of Elimelek, Kilion, and Mahlon. I have also acquired Ruth the Moabite, Mahlon's widow, as my wife, in order to maintain the name of the dead with his property, so that his name will not disappear from among his family or from his hometown. Today you are witnesses!" (Ruth 4:9–10)

While I might bristle at his acquisitional language of Ruth, looking beyond the cultural restrictions, I see how Ruth's first-chapter loyalty invited Boaz's last-chapter loyalty. He might have the societal authority, but it was her influence that changed this story. He then offered her relationship and presence, and we see their bond as secure. Both Boaz and Ruth were seen, soothed, safe, and secure, exchanging with each other the gifts that come from first being seen, soothed, safe, and secure in God. Their union would purify and clarify their hearts. This was how it worked; they would have biblical storylines that rival any we read, but their greatest adventure would be learning how to keep their two planks up against each other.

God is a restorer, a redeemer, and a rescuer. He is a reconciler; He repairs. Naomi changed her name to "Bitter," thinking God was punishing her, but He wasn't stuck in the day she was living. He saw her whole life at one time and knew how He would encourage Ruth to exercise her ezer-ness, offering help that would lead to the redemption of her whole family. This is what He does. Ruth had a past relationship she brought into the marriage; Boaz had interesting parents (one was a probable spy, the other a former prostitute). They were from different cultural backgrounds, and yet … God brought them together. This remarkable God then used their relational nature to give them a shared adventure we are still talking about today.

Security is powerful; it answers our questions, gives confidence, and breeds attachment. Todd and I formalized the adoption of a young woman who had been living with us for years. Dee Dee was twenty-three at the time of her adoption, although we considered her a daughter for a long season beforehand. Getting a chance to legalize this relationship was a celebratory occasion, and our large, noisy extended family walked into the courtroom ready for a party.

I apologized to the judge for our disruptive presence, but he said, "Don't worry about making noise. Adoption court has a unique atmosphere. It's not as formal as you might imagine a courtroom. You can laugh, cry, and express whatever emotions you are having. If the attorneys and I don't join you, don't be offended. It's not that we aren't moved, but this is our job and we do it all day long."

The proceedings went as you might imagine: an attorney reported on her work with us, Dee Dee declared this was her will, and it was time for Todd and me to share our declaration of intent—we wanted this relationship made permanent. We prepared the following blessing to read into the court record.

> *Dear Dee,*
>
> *This day we are formalizing what has long already been true: you are a Guckenberger and all that that means. You are an invitational, Jesus-loving, up-for-fun addition to this family. Our earliest memories of you were at track meets and basketball games, and we look back now and realize God had you already standing out*

to us in Technicolor. In all the kinds of ways that are hard to explain to anyone outside, you felt like family as soon as you arrived.

As your mom famously tells everyone: it doesn't matter where you came from; it matters where you belong ... and in front of these witnesses, I want you to hear me say: you belong with us. There is a lot we love about you: your humor, your walk with Jesus, your sincerity, your love for the whole family (grandparents, nieces, sisters, little brothers, etc.). You are kind, dynamic, special, gifted, and we look forward to a lifetime of loving you.

You were a puzzle piece we didn't know we were missing until you filled us in. We see you ... you are our daughter. You are their sister. You are an aunt, a granddaughter, and a cousin. So hear and receive this blessing from Numbers 6:24–26: "[May] the LORD *bless you and keep you; the* LORD *make his face shine on you and be gracious to you; the* LORD *turn his face toward you and give you peace."*

In the same way we are giving you our name, God gives His name to His kids. We love you, Dee Dee Nicole Guckenberger.

Somewhere in the middle of it, I heard a sniffling noise behind me. I turned to see the judge and attorney in tears. *"Right?"* I said to them. *"This is so good.* Be our witness: she is seen, soothed, safe, and secure, first by God, and now by us."

Neither Dee Dee nor Todd or I needed to guard our emotions. We didn't have to hide or control the narrative; the utter extravagance of love that day was almost embarrassing to watch. We were as crazy about her as she was about us. It was a picture of what it looked like when the shepherd found the lost sheep or the father of the prodigal ran to his son. We invited her to be permanently under our tree and she said yes, so now nothing will ever be the same. John 10:28 says, "I give them eternal life, and they shall never perish; no one will snatch them out of my hand." We hold on to Dee because He holds on to us. And in the end, we all benefit from that love exchange.

Ruth experienced the same blessing:

> Then the elders and all the people at the gate said, "We are wit-
> nesses. May the LORD make the woman who is coming into your
> home like Rachel and Leah, who together built up the family
> of Israel. May you have standing in Ephrathah and be famous
> in Bethlehem. Through the offspring the LORD gives you by
> this young woman, may your family be like that of Perez, whom
> Tamar bore to Judah."
>
> So Boaz took Ruth and she became his wife. When he made
> love to her, the LORD enabled her to conceive, and she gave birth
> to a son. The women said to Naomi: "Praise be to the LORD, who
> this day has not left you without a guardian-redeemer. May he
> become famous throughout Israel! He will renew your life and
> sustain you in your old age. For your daughter-in-law, who loves
> you and who is better to you than seven sons, has given him
> birth." (Ruth 4:11–15)

God loves to tell redemption stories. He did it with Ruth, He did it with Dee
Dee, and He does it all day long in every corner of the earth. He wants to partner
with us and give back to His children what was taken. We might get stuck on a
particular day, focused on what's not happening or what's missing, but my prayer is
that my eyes are lifted to see what God is doing in our families.

What is He causing us to see? Who does He want us to soothe? Where can we
offer safety and security to someone in His name? Where can we be generous with
our presence?

Ruth's story teaches us God is always doing more than one thing at a time.
He was doing something for Ruth, for Naomi, and for Boaz. He was doing
something for other widows watching and for Boaz's workers learning. Ruth and
Boaz would go on to have a son named Obed, whom God had a plan for in their
coming together. God was doing something for their future grandson Jesse and

great-grandson David, who picked up a stone and slew a giant. When we ezer, as Ruth did, we obediently give over our lives to His plans. We can only trust that He is at work and is writing the best stories.

Questions to Consider

When was a time you went to God feeling rejected?

What part of Ruth's story moves you?

Where can you offer safety and security to someone in His name?

Journal

Who is someone who really sees you?

Chapter 21

How far can an ezer stretch and not break?

I remember everything about *the day*. Anyone with a cancer diagnosis in their family knows what I mean. The day in your life that divides all events from there on out to be referenced as "before the day" or "after the day." For me, it was finding out my dad had cancer.

I wouldn't have been able to tell you that night, or even still a hundred nights later, that I was in pain. A shot went off at some starting gate—the adrenaline was so strong—and I felt more like I was beginning a race than suffering devastation. I didn't even know where I was running (toward a happy ending, I am sure), but I know it felt good to be on the move. We were active and united fighting an ugly beast I had been certain was never supposed to come to our house. God would protect us, right? Isn't that what the Bible said?

When I look back on that year, the memories are unusually intense. To a casual observer, they could sound almost pleasant. We stopped all nonessential activities. We cherished time together and planned extraordinarily meaningful family events. We were available to one another in unprecedented ways. We prayed and worshipped and read like our lives depended on it, or at least like my dad's life did.

"The counts are lower!"

"The cancer is spreading."

"The doctor said he was a candidate!"

"The chemo isn't working."

I didn't want to admit it at the time, but I was still clinging to a childish faith, one where the score was always settled in my favor and God always came through (how I asked Him to). I had a strong faith in God, but I had fashioned Him into something He wasn't. I now reference that time as my "genie God" days. I hoped by rubbing His belly, I could produce a God who would grant my wishes. Of course, I never said it like that. I said all things would work out if I prayed where two or three were gathered, or if I prayed with holy oil, or if I, as a resident of God's kingdom on earth, prayed and rejected the illness. Doesn't matter how I said it, what I meant was, *God, if You really love us, You will stop this.* What I didn't say, but equally meant, was, *And if You don't stop this, I am not sure I can believe in You.*

So to whom will you compare me, the Incomparable?
    Can you picture me without reducing me?
People with a lot of money
    hire craftsmen to make them gods.
The artisan delivers the god,
    and they kneel and worship it!
They carry it around in holy parades,
    then take it home and put it on a shelf.
And there it sits, day in and day out,
    a dependable god, always right where you put it.
Say anything you want to it, it never talks back.
    Of course, it never *does* anything either!
Think about this. Wrap your minds around it.
    This is serious business, rebels. Take it to heart.
        (Isaiah 46:5–8 MSG)

As the year wore on, Dad only got sicker. But I still knew my God would save the day; He always did. I thought my dad knew that as well, so I was surprised when he began to prepare me for his death. Now that I'm a parent, I realize he was trying his hardest to use his final days to convince me this was not a situation without hope. And hope could maybe be in something higher than a clean bill of health.

That last week of his life, a relative called him from out of town. He urged her to come right then while he could still see her, instead of traveling for the funeral. It was a Monday afternoon when she arrived, and I excused myself from the room so they could have some time alone. After about an hour she left, and I could see her eyes were red from crying. I walked into the hospital room, expecting to see him wiped out from that long exchange, and instead, he was animated. "Beth, it will all be worth it if she comes to the kingdom with us." He looked at me, willing me to understand.

#$%@#? All worth it? What planet was he living on? I could think of no circumstance that would make the last year "worth it." I wish I had seen then what he was modeling for me. It would have made that exchange all the sweeter, and I might have even joined him. Jeremiah 15:19 says, "And if you extract the precious from the worthless, you will become My spokesman" (NASB). But he (whose mind was set on things above) was the only one between the two of us who could see the higher value of her salvation.

Just a week later, we all gathered around his bed for his last night with us. I was holding on to more than his hand. I was holding on to pretense—a false assumption I had made along the way—that if all my stories didn't end as I wished them, then God had somehow failed me.

"Absent from the body means present with the Lord." My mom whispered Paul's words from 2 Corinthians. And then suddenly, eternity for me had an address. It became a place instead of a concept. It was real, and Dad now lived there.

Truthfully, my grieving wasn't very pretty. I had all the normal stages, including anger. But my childish faith died next to his earthly body, and in its place was born a dynamic faith. I learned God could handle my questions and my doubts because He is unchanging and perfect and wholly sure of Himself. I have grown to appreciate His patience with my questions, almost as much as the perfectness of His answers.

Until we grow, we cannot help but store our faith in a frame. When God operates outside of what we can understand or explain away, we are faced with two choices: dismiss that action as either false or unloving, or grow our frame and our understanding of what He is capable of.

I had made God into something He was not—a personal magician I could coax into doing tricks for me. Today, I am vastly more exposed to needs that are painful and circumstances not easily solved, and now I believe in a bigger God—one who has our whole lives in His hands and whose timing is different from mine. Could God be more than a chronological order of days? Could His story have started long before I arrived and still be going on after its perceived end?

I could try to explain my dad's death with layers of stories that came in the season following the funeral, but that doesn't feel right. I know God could have touched those lives in lots of ways without killing off my dad to do it. Rather, we live in a world that has been broken—physically and spiritually. God could have pulled His hands off and watched it spiral out of control with sin, disease, pain, and war. Instead, He intervenes, redeems what is happening, and uses situations regardless of their causes for His greater good and the good of those bearing witness to it.

When I intersect with a situation that I find too hard to carry, I remember I'm seeing it from a single point in time and things are occurring around that point that will culminate in the next chapter.

I talked to a parent this week whose child is being hospitalized and most likely won't ever come home again. It was a heartbreaking conversation; he cried, and I cried. I wanted to be an ezer at that moment, to offer help, but what kind of help do we offer when it's not within our power to change a story heading in a direction we don't like and can't control? It's not okay, it doesn't feel good, and there aren't easy answers, but in the end, I encouraged that father to hold on to hope ...

What exactly is hope? And how do we hold on to it when it can seem like life is getting harder and the Order of Brokenness we live in is worse than ever?! As we define hope, it might be tempting to think of hope as a feeling that something desirable is likely to happen.

I hope it doesn't rain. I hope I get a raise.

But unlike a wish, hope implies the expectation of obtaining what is desired. The word for "hope" in Hebrew is *tikvah*, which is defined as "a cord, expectation, and hope." Hope is something to hold on to ... in English it's abstract, but hope in Hebrew is a strong visual: a cord. Hope is a rope!

How well we hold on to that rope can be tempting to think of in terms of personality. *I am optimistic, or I am a pessimist.* We can describe ourselves as "cup half full" or "cup half empty" people.

The story of God's kids is a story of hope, about people who believe there is always more going on than what we see, and despite what we experience on earth, we believe the cup is *meant* to be full. And no matter what happens, this cup *will be full again.*

This is why we have hope. This is the rope, the hope we hold on to.

These muscles don't develop overnight. While they're being built, it's important to not try to put our best foot forward with Jesus, pretend, or have a false sense of hope or faith. He knows our hearts, He knows when we are confused, disappointed, or hurt. The Bible holds space for people to speak the truth, to mourn. One of the books dedicated to having hope when you are hurting is Lamentations.

> I remember my affliction and my wandering,
>   the bitterness and the gall.
> I well remember them,
>   and my soul is downcast within me. (Lamentations 3:19–20)

My favorite part about this passage is the honesty of the writer, Jeremiah. Our version today might sound like, "I remember the death of my friend, my lost job, my health crisis ... and my soul is downcast." We don't have to pretend, because God honors our lamenting. Some of the best help we offer as ezers is doing the same.

> Yet this I call to mind
>   and therefore I have hope. (verse 21)

The Bible addresses the need for this battle for hope to start with our minds: setting our minds on things above, taking every thought captive, renewing our thinking ... What are we remembering when our souls are downcast? If it's true, then *therefore* I have hope. In the infinite love of God, we can be anywhere, in any circumstance, and just thinking about Him can restore rest and hope. It's not something He passes out sparingly, or that I must earn. It's given freely to those He has chosen as His kids. I am made for this kind of love, and even if I don't want it, my heart betrays me. I am made for this kind of spiritual intimacy, to be the object of His affection.

I am made for this kind of love, and even if I don't want it, my heart betrays me.

> Because of the LORD's great love we are not consumed,
>   for his compassions never fail. (verse 22)

He is always with us, and He never tires of us. We can lament and not despair. His way is compassion, and it never fails. We understand that God will save us from our sins and we will one day spend eternity with Him, but it's easy to forget that in the here and now He wants to heal us, He wants to protect us from being *consumed*.

> They are new every morning;
> great is your faithfulness. (verse 23)

New every morning? He isn't human, like running out saying, *"This? Again?"* When I think about the hardest stories I carry, there comes a point in the evening when I can't hold it together anymore; it can feel like too much. It's crazy to me that He designed our body systems to wear out, then need sleep, but in the morning be renewed. This new deposit of His faithfulness brings with it the unintended benefit of contentment. I don't need to strive; I can utterly count on more of what I need to be on its way.

> I say to myself, "The LORD is my portion;
> therefore I will wait for him." (verse 24)

"I say to myself…" What does my self-talk sound like? The writer said the Lord was his portion. Self-talk is critical and directly tied to how we were once spoken to. In the middle of this (whatever "this" is), He is enough. He is my portion. I will wait, believe, and trust until the cup fills, even if I don't see it. Prayer with Him, then, is the ultimate act of vulnerability, the lying open of my heart for Him to see and tinker with. My guard is down, and I am my truest self; here's my brokenness, here are my dreams, here's my desire. I am waiting …

> The LORD is good to those whose hope is in him,
> to the one who seeks him;
> it is good to wait quietly
> for the salvation of the LORD. (verses 25–26)

See the pattern? A lot of hoping ends up looking like seeking and waiting. It isn't crossing our fingers, closing our eyes, and giving up, or making bargains or deals with God. It's seeking and waiting. And in that waiting, it's believing He is still in pursuit of my best and His perfect will. I get in trouble when I think He must be busy with something else, or what I'm waiting for isn't a priority for Him, or worst of all, that my idea of next steps is better than His. *So why doesn't He just hurry up and do as I asked? He says it's good for me to "wait quietly"?* I do wonder why, but it must be something to do with His understanding of what I really desire versus what I think I desire. That's the benefit of having a perfect Lover of my soul: He knows me better than I know myself.

> For no one is cast off
> by the Lord forever.
> Though he brings grief, he will show compassion,
> so great is his unfailing love.
> For he does not willingly bring affliction
> or grief to anyone. (verses 31–33)

We can't miss that last verse, "For he does not willingly bring affliction or grief to anyone." He has big shoulders and has been accused of all kinds of things by His kids: *How could You let this happen? If You loved me, then why ...?*

I've had those questions—moments of utter irritation with God and a distaste for what He's allowed. But I can't sit there long; it's not good for our relationship. I have to ask Him to penetrate my broken soul with this truth: "He does not willingly bring affliction or grief to anyone."

He is crazy about us, and His heart breaks with ours. He came to make all things new. He isn't looking to be nice to me or do me a favor or give me a treat. This is the only story that counts. And in my selfish nature, I can prefer all three of those to His perfect will. I am prone to want what I want when I want it. So, I call (this truth) to mind and therefore have and hold on to hope.

He will strengthen us with power (Ephesians 3:14–16).

He will give us rest (Matthew 11:28).

He will supply all our needs (Philippians 4:9).

He will cause everything to work together for the good of those who love Him (Romans 8:28).

He will not abandon us (Joshua 1:5).

He will not be separate from us (Romans 8:38–39).

He who promised is faithful (Hebrews 10:23).

May *this* be our self-talk.

Questions to Consider

How have you treated God as your personal genie?

When was a time God stretched your faith frame?

Which truth in Lamentations 3 most moved you?

Journal

Is there something you sense you need to lament?

Chapter 22

What do ezers do with their desire for bacon?

Have you ever wanted what you couldn't have? *I have.*

Have you ever wavered in your faith? *I have.*

Has something bitter tasted sweet to you? *Unfortunately.*

When you sensed God's leading to go right, where did you turn? *Left.*

We assume a warrior must be uncompromising, but that's a tall order. Most days I am well-intentioned yet still a sinful, fleshly vessel with a Spirit-filled core. I understand compromise. I stand in a long line of people whom God has called into battle yet have known they weren't *enough*. In the end, He simply asks for our obedience. How He adds it all up and counts it is up to Him. It's what makes the following illustration so poignant.

The Sorek Valley, and specifically Bet Shemesh, is a location in Israel where the stories of Samson occurred—including the loss and eventual recovery of the Ark of the Covenant—with the Philistines. Recorded in 1 Samuel chapters 4 and 6, both stories involve the entrapment of the pagan Philistine culture.

When archaeologists excavated the site of Bet Shemesh, they dug through the layers of a tel, a large hill that has built up over several centuries of occupation. In almost every level of civilization they encountered, they found pig bones in the debris.[33] Since God forbade pigs to be eaten, this was evidence of compromise by some in the Hebrew faith. These were God's kids, half of them His ezers. How could they compromise and still be effective? The natural consequence of disobedience is the loss of opportunity to impact the kingdom.

These Israelites were failing to be true to God's commandments and adopting the lifestyle of the nearby pagan nations. It's easy to judge their choices and assume they deserved to be captured or defeated because of their sin, but before I go too far down that road, I ask myself: *Where are* my *pig bones*? Are they in my wallet? Browser history? Recycling bin? Social media accounts? Where can you see evidence I have adopted a worldly culture and compromised my Christian walk? Or used my strengths for the wrong kingdom? Can an ezer dabble in the world a little bit, eat some bacon, and still be effective for the kingdom?

The Bible uses the expression "kicking against the goads," a rural image, to illustrate our struggle to settle into God's will and ways. Farmers "goad" their oxen in the field, urging a stubborn animal into motion with a goad, a slender piece of timber. When an ox kicks against it, it causes itself injury and pain. Ecclesiastes 12:11 says God's words are "like goads ... like firmly embedded nails" that prod us. *Ox goad* in Hebrew means literally "the thing that teaches." Sometimes the very thing that hurts us is the instrument God will use for our good.

God asked Saul why he was kicking against the goads in Acts 26:14: "We all fell to the ground, and I heard a voice saying to me in Aramaic, 'Saul, Saul, why do you persecute me? It is hard for you to kick against the goads.'" He was telling Saul that He had been trying to get him to go where He was prodding, and he wouldn't go.

Saul had heard Stephen speak, yet he did not listen—he continued to kick against the goads—and persecuted every Christian he could find. God finally stopped him by speaking to him from heaven and put him in darkness for three days (like Jonah). We can resist God and His ways, but we end up only hurting ourselves. It's futile to "kick against the goads" and points to how out of touch our own hearts can get, which were designed to want what God offers.

I've kicked against my own goads when God has said "Stop" and I've responded with "Just a little more ..." When God has used a goad on me, it was because He was trying to guide and protect me from my willfulness. The most important thing I have as an ezer is my heart, the "wellspring of life" (Proverbs 4:23 WEB), and God goads to keep me from its destruction, even while I simultaneously complain about it.

Shame over pig bones or goad scars has held back many ezers. Some shame comes from external sources—people who look at our lives and choices and want us to feel bad about ourselves so they can feel good about theirs. Other times, I can muster up shame just fine on my own, when I forget that shame separates and defeats me, driving me toward isolation.

It's where I start to think things like, *If they really knew what I am/do/think ...* or *If I can protect this (whatever* this *is), then I am safe.* Isolation is fertile ground for distorted thinking. It allows lies to linger and pig bones to pile up. It's in a vulnerable community that I can confess my sins, request accountability, make mistakes, and ask questions. This silences the enemy, who taunts me. The emotions I feel are not to be pushed away or shamed. They are to be attended to by the Holy Spirit, in the presence of healthy fellowship, in the quietness of my heart, so what's really happening, *the meaning* behind my behavior, can be exposed.

John tells a story about a woman caught in adultery:

> Jesus returned to the Mount of Olives, but early the next morning he was back again at the Temple. A crowd soon gathered, and he sat down and taught them. As he was speaking, the teachers of religious law and the Pharisees brought a woman who had been caught in the act of adultery. They put her in front of the crowd. (John 8:1–3 NLT)

First of all, a man also had to be involved. (Now, where is *he?*) Legally speaking, the standard of evidence was very high for this crime. There had to be two witnesses who agreed perfectly. They had to see the sexual acts take place; it wasn't enough to see the pair leaving the same room together or even lying in the same bed. So under these conditions, evidence of adultery would be almost impossible unless it was a setup. Maybe the man was in on it and used the woman as a pawn in his conflict against Jesus.

Now, take a minute to imagine how the woman felt when it sunk in … it would have been her darkest hour.

> "Teacher," they said to Jesus, "this woman was caught in the act
> of adultery. The law of Moses says to stone her. What do you say?"
> (verses 4–5 NLT)

What do you say? What does Jesus say when we are caught in our worst moments? How do you picture Him looking at you? If Jesus said, "Let her go," then He would seem to break the Law of Moses and relax public morals. If He said, "Execute her for the crime of adultery," then Jesus would seem harsh and cruel.

He always has another way.

The phrase *tikkun olam* in Hebrew means "to heal or repair the world, to make what is crooked, straight." It is a Jewish principle telling us to do what we can to help make broken things whole. God's design is to use us, created in His image, to act as His priests in this world. It's the work of an ezer to be on the lookout for moments just like this when everything seems upside down and it's easier to look away or pretend you didn't see it or, worse yet, stare while doing nothing. When an ezer comes into a scene, the questions she must ask are, *Where can I help? What is crooked?* and *How can I straighten it out?*

When an ezer comes into a scene,
the questions she must ask are,
Where can I help? What is crooked?
and *How can I straighten it out?*

I have a T-shirt that says, "Make the world suck less, do good." I call it my *tik-kun olam* shirt and wear it as a reminder that I have choices when I'm confronted with someone who isn't acting according to God's design. I can criticize or lead. Stacy Reed responded to me online, writing, "Being a warrior means we have access to power within us to right the wrongs we see, to meet needs when we can, to fight for injustices to be righted, to change the world, to be a voice for the vulnerable people around us." If I am seduced by pig bones, I am unable to *tikkun olam*; I am consumed with myself and my sin.

> They were trying to trap him into saying something they could
> use against him, but Jesus stooped down and wrote in the dust
> with his finger. (verse 6 NLT)

Every act of Jesus was on purpose. Anything that doesn't make sense has context somewhere in the text. For example, Jesus' comment about forgiving "seven times seventy" is a direct reference to Lamech in Genesis 4:23–24: "Lamech said to his wives, 'Adah and Zillah, listen to me; wives of Lamech, hear my words. I have killed a man for wounding me, a young man for injuring me. If Cain is avenged seven times, then Lamech seventy-seven times.'" Jesus was saying, if the sons of man were known for vengeance seven times seventy, then the children of God would be known for forgiveness seven times seventy ... Following this logic, if He bent to write in the dust, there must be a verse somewhere about dust writing, and finding it will unlock meaning for this John 8 passage.

"LORD, you are the hope of Israel; all who forsake you will be put to shame. Those who turn away from you will be written in the dust because they have forsaken the LORD, the spring of living water" (Jeremiah 17:13). I've heard plenty of messages about Jesus drawing attention away from the woman, and for sure He did that, but also He was counting on that audience not wanting their names written in that dust. They thought they were putting Jesus to the test, but it was the other way around. The difference between "test" and "tempt" is found in the tester's motivations. The devil tempts so we sin. God tests to sharpen our character, with no focus on making His kids fail. He was teaching them how to treat Him.

Jesus is always the teacher, and here He was teaching the woman (I *see* you ...), He was teaching the accusers (Look into your *own* heart ...), and all of us He knew would later read about the account—what is He teaching us?

To some of us, He's saying, *Put down your stones.*

And to others, *You are more than the sum of your acts.*

> They kept demanding an answer, so he stood up again and said, "All right, but let the one who has never sinned throw the first stone!" Then he stooped down again and wrote in the dust. (John 8:7–8 NLT)

He was stooped and then stood up against them ... looked them in the eye. Those details matter. He, YAHWEH, is willing to stand up to our accuser: our enemy. Revelation 12:10 calls Satan the "accuser of our brothers and sisters," and John 8:44, "He was a murderer from the beginning, and does not stand in the truth, because there is no truth in him. When he lies, he speaks out of his own character, for he is a liar and the father of lies" (ESV). This enemy lies to us. He tells us things about ourselves that aren't true. He cloaks us in darkness. He might have been whispering to the woman that she was worthless or this would forever define her. He wants us to hide in the darkness, to stay in stasis because of our shame.

Her accusers had perceived political and popular cultural power, but Jesus stood up to them. He doesn't just have power; He *is* power. He will share it with us. Don't miss this moment: He is strong, confident, and powerful. He isn't letting anyone get away with anything. Ezer, this is our invitation, because we are made in His image. Stand in front of the accusers and defend the broken. This takes a fierceness we can't just suddenly muster up when we need it; we must train to be simultaneously gentle and strong.

When the accusers heard this, they slipped away one by one, beginning with the oldest, until only Jesus was left in the middle of the crowd with the woman. (John 8:9 NLT)

And now we are back to the beginning of the story, so what do You say, Jesus? She's alone with Him and what does He say? What does it look like when He sees our pig bones? *What do we think Jesus says to us when we are alone with Him?*

> I am faithful and just and will forgive your sins and cleanse you
> from all unrighteousness (1 John 1:9).
> I am not here to condemn the world, but so the world might be
> saved (John 3:16).
> I will have compassion on you, treading your sin underfoot. I will
> cast your sins into the depths of the sea (Micah 7:19).
> There is therefore now no condemnation for My kids (Romans 8:1).

He says: Step out of the darkness. I do not condemn you. Go and sin no more. And if *He* doesn't condemn us, neither can anyone else. We might think we are out of the story because of a choice we have made. But think of Peter, who denied Christ three times. God knew the story that was to come for Peter in Acts 2 and Pentecost. He has good stories still ahead for us; we are not the sum of our worst mistakes. If someone is treating you poorly, you might have to teach them to treat you as a daughter of the King.

God is in the details and will show up for us, whether in dust writing or garbage heaps. We can respond to His invitation of holiness. He's offering us the same grace as the woman in John 8; we can receive it and live differently, or sit still, frozen in our shame.

Christianity is a story, much more than it is a religion, and since it's a story, there is an Author. He is the source of all the good, and all the adventure and desire our hearts long for.

C. S. Lewis wrote, "If you consider the unblushing promises of reward and the staggering nature of the rewards promised in the Gospels, it would seem that Our Lord finds your desires not too strong, but too weak."[34]

There is an enemy who hates this heart of ours, so he distorts our desires and wants our destruction. The battle between them and the invitation to fight in it is the whole meaning of our lives. Sometimes, when we see an artist's rendering of spiritual warfare, God is represented as the same size as Satan; however, these are not characters of the same size. This enemy has to submit to the spiritual reality that he doesn't have God's power. Because of the birthright we have as co-heirs with Christ, we can fight with confidence, expecting the opposition and yet ready to celebrate the victory.

Questions to Consider

What was the result of Saul's kicking against the goads?

What do you think God is saying to you when you are caught in your worst moment?

What can we do when we want some bacon?

Journal

Where are your pig bones?

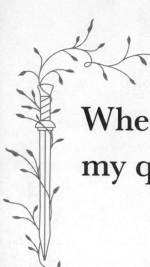

Chapter 23

Where do I go with my questions?

I was speaking at a conference for missionaries who had been in the field for over thirty-five years. In front of almost a thousand attendees I admitted, "Maybe this is how a sports enthusiast would feel at a hall of fame event, or an artist at the Oscars ... but you are the coolest collection of people I have ever seen gathered." I meant it, for I knew I had much to learn from the lessons represented by each of their lives.

During the breaks, I would wander around and ask, "What do you have for me? What have you seen and learned?" This spurred many good conversations, and I soaked up their meaningful responses, but one stood out.

Tilting his head, a man looked at me and said, "It was a good fight."

This landed *right* in my soul. He wasn't pretending it had been easy; it *had* been a fight, but it had been a good fight, and this encouraged me. His response implied not waiting until things were better, or he was whole, or he had what he needed. The very word *fight* implicated the utter uphillness of it all. God invites us to engage while our faith is still being worked out with fear and trembling, while we are still being healed. This is part of the reason it's a fight. We are in our own battles, and at the same time, we take on another's.

I can be busy fighting the battle, confessing my sin, asking Jesus for what I need, and advancing the kingdom the best I know how, and then when I hit a hurdle, my first reaction is usually to question.

Why did that have to happen? Why couldn't You have done something? When will You make it right? How will You make it right? Why does it have to be so hard? So confusing? Hey, are You listening?

Some questions don't have good answers. And the futile search to make sense of what we cannot understand, nor were we ever designed to understand, can prevent even the boldest ezer from doing what she was created to do: *help*. It makes women who are utterly convinced this world is about the One to come some of the most dangerous women on the planet. They understand at the soul level that to lose your life is to gain it. They don't need to see the three-year plan, or to understand all the steps between here and there; they just embrace the unknown of this spiritual adventure and love as liberally as they can all along the way.

My younger brother was in high school when our father died. My older brother and I made a covenant with each other that we would "show up" for Ben for the life events my dad would now miss—graduations, weddings, moves—and we did. For the last twenty-five years, we have cheered on degree completions and the births of his children. So, when his beautiful wife was diagnosed with cancer in her thirties, we showed up, but I also came with all my questions. *Why is this happening to his family?*

Those questions can function like brakes on my warrioring if I am not careful. I am allowed to ask them, but I can't let them slow me down.

We prayed for and listened to them as Ben's wife waged war against this disease, and our collective hearts broke when God decided to take her home. I still have *all the questions* about this for God. I know in the end the answers are based on His sovereignty and ultimate healing of her. But I still have lots and lots of questions about this and a dozen other stories I don't like and can't understand. Those questions can function like brakes on my warrioring if I am not careful. I am allowed to ask them, but I can't let them slow me down.

Jesus liked a good question too. He is recorded as having asked a lot of questions, the kinds that stir the soul.

> If you love those who love you, what reward will you get? (Matthew 5:46)
>
> Who of you by worrying can add a single hour to your life? (Matthew 6:27; Luke 12:25)
>
> Why do you look at the speck of sawdust in your brother's eye and pay no attention to the plank in your own eye? (Matthew 7:3)
>
> Why are you so afraid? (Matthew 8:26; Mark 4:40)
>
> Do you believe that I am able to do this? (Matthew 9:28)
>
> Why did you doubt? (Matthew 14:31; Luke 24:38)
>
> How many loaves do you have? (Matthew 15:34)
>
> Who do you say I am? (Matthew 16:15)
>
> What good will it be for someone to gain the whole world, yet forfeit their soul? Or what can anyone give in exchange for their soul? (Matthew 16:26)
>
> What do you think? If a man owns a hundred sheep, and one of them wanders away, will he not leave the ninety-nine on the hills and go to look for the one that wandered off? (Matthew 18:12; Luke 15:4)
>
> Why do you ask me about what is good? (Matthew 19:17)
>
> What is it you want? (Matthew 20:21, 32)

Do you bring in a lamp to put it under a bowl or a bed? Instead, don't you put it on its stand? (Mark 4:21)

What do you want me to do for you? (Mark 10:51; John 1:38)

Are you asleep? (Mark 14:37)

Why are you thinking these things in your hearts? (Luke 5:22)

Why do you call me, "Lord, Lord," and do not do what I say? (Luke 6:46)

Where is your faith? (Luke 8:25)

Do you want to get well? (John 5:6)

Have I not chosen you? (John 6:70)

If I am telling the truth, why don't you believe me? (John 8:46; 11:26)

Do you understand what I have done for you? (John 13:12)

Do you love me? (John 21:17)

I know Jesus is fine with questions, and I know He likes the exchange that happens when I think about His and ask my own. They require me to engage in a relationship with God versus exercising religion. He wants the conversation and understands the growth that results from introspection and, ultimately, repentance. Breakthrough and healing are available when the thief has wreaked havoc on me, or I didn't do what the Shepherd said, *or* I believed what the Shepherd told me. This is a resurrection gospel at its core, and even when there is loss, the story isn't over yet.

Jesus learned this technique from His Father, who also asked a lot of questions.

Where are you? Who told you that you were naked? (Genesis 3:9, 11)

What have you done? (Genesis 4:10)

Why did you despise the word of the LORD by doing what is evil in his eyes? (2 Samuel 12:9)

Whom shall I send? And who will go for us? (Isaiah 6:8)

These questions were always to get to the heart of the matter with one of His kids who needed redirection. Questions don't need to be brakes; they can turn into arrows.

When I wonder what God is saying to me, I revisit this list and answer Him. *Yes, I want to be well. This is who I say You are. I don't want to worry, I am sorry. I do understand what You've done. No, I am not asleep. This is what I am afraid of ...* I offer up to God my angst or anger, and He gives me back His peace and grace. That is how we refuel. Or how I've gotten over spiritual hurdles and unanswerable questions like why someone I love died. I am not so much looking for an answer as I am looking for comfort. That's offered when I turn to God and see Him face to face and I can be reminded that while it's not easy, *it's a good fight.* I might give my heart over to someone or something other than God; that's called sin, or even addiction. It happens in a careless or even desperate moment, but all the while, He just waits and never moves unless it's to come toward me.

Sometimes, the calling God has for us to help is big, and we need Him to lighten the load. Typically, when we feel stressed, we talk of feeling "burdened" or "weighed down." I can think of many times on the front lines of my life when I felt weighed or pressed down. I am feeling it today, even as I write. I have an adoptive son who is struggling to become a young adult. This battle wearies me, and I can feel "heavy" with questions.

In Hebrew, a different picture is used for the same idea. The word for "distress" is *tzar* or *tzarah*, and it also means "narrow" or "tight." The picture is that of being hemmed in, squeezed, or trapped with no options. King David often spoke about being pressed, *tzarah*, by his enemies. Don't we all know what it means to feel "squeezed" by something?

God wants to provide relief (*rahav* in Hebrew) for His ezers. *Rahav* means "widening." Consider these verses where we read of God's compassion toward the pressure we can feel.

> He brought me out into a spacious place;
>> he rescued me because he delighted in me. (2 Samuel 22:20)

You have set my feet in a wide place. (Psalm 31:8 NKJV)

From my distress I called upon the LORD;
The LORD answered me and set me in a large place. (Ps. 118:5 NASB)

Though I am hemmed in (*tzarah*), you will lead me into a wide,
    open place (lit., you will widen, *rahav*, me).
Have mercy on me and respond to my prayer. (Psalm 4:1–2 NET)

He isn't sitting back, watching us struggle with a fight we don't want to be in, carrying a load too heavy, or in a stressful assignment with more questions than answers. He wants to provide us relief, to widen the space. Now when I feel squeezed, I pray, "Lead me into a wide space ..." This is more than the daily routine of spiritual disciplines. It's the lifeline we hold on to when everything feels *too much*.

Our circumstances might not change, but how we manage our emotions, peace, and minds amid those circumstances is critical. Being in a wide space does not mean the diagnosis changes or we get a raise or our prodigal returns or everything suddenly makes sense. Being in a wide space is about what we get from Jesus while we are "helping," and what we give to Jesus amid the pressure we feel. This kind of exchange is critical for what He's asking of us. He's right there with us.

The gospel truth is intended to give us the freedom to love both God and the whole world. When I ignore how my heart is feeling squeezed and attempt to follow doctrine or spiritual habits, or will it away, or shame myself into trying to feel something other than what I am, I lose the very heart Jesus died to save. My passion drains and my purpose turns into checklists and programs, instead of people and adventure.

Consider this passage in Isaiah 63: "In all their distress (*tzar*) he too was distressed, and the angel of his presence saved them. In his love and mercy he redeemed them; he lifted them up and carried them all the days of old" (verse 9).

When I feel like it's *all too much*, I tend to imagine God sadly shaking His head at me and saying, "Are you stuck again?" But what if that's the wrong image? What if instead He wants to offer me His presence and redeem me? To carry me? This verse teaches when God's people were distressed and afflicted (*tzar*), He Himself was afflicted (*tzar*). God wasn't relaxing comfortably in heaven while His people were in distress. When we are squeezed into a tight spot, God feels squeezed too! He is always intimately near and ready to engage us in our questions with unending grace.

Questions to Consider

What questions do you have for God?

Which of the listed questions Jesus asked is hardest for you to answer?

When do you put results above obedience?

Journal

When you are distressed, what do you imagine God is saying to you?

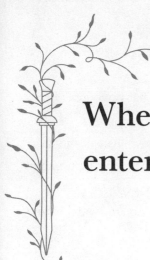

Chapter 24

When should an ezer enter another's chaos?

I woke up to speak in a church where, the night before, the community had experienced a terrible shooting. Several people had died in a local bar, including some innocent bystanders. I knew it would be on everyone's mind that morning, and even though I already had something planned, I wondered what I could say that would be meaningful to a congregation that was both sad and mad about what had happened in their city.

I walked out and put five objects on a table: a water bottle, a small fan, my Bible, a tree branch, and an apple. I began by referencing the current events we all woke up to, and wondering with them how we should respond. This type of concern isn't new; it's part of countless tragic stories throughout history. If we can learn these five reoccurring elements, we can predict the pattern and discern what God is asking of us.

I explained the reason for the objects:

The water bottle symbolized **chaos**. There is always a problem, a sin, a crisis, in the beginning. Throughout the Scriptures, water represents chaos, starting with the chaotic waters of creation.

The fan represented the **hovering Spirit**. God is near the chaos, ready to engage. The word for "wind" in Hebrew is *rûah*, and the word for "Spirit" in

Hebrew is *rûah*. It was my best attempt to symbolize the Holy Spirit as it hovers over, then enters the chaos.

The Bible represented **God speaking**, His very words. He has wisdom, direction, conviction, and words to share with those listening.

The tree branch, just taken from the parking lot landscape, equated to an olive branch representing peace, or **shalom**, in Hebrew. In the aftermath of God speaking, peace breaks out. Every time.

The apple is the age-old symbol of **temptation**. An invitation to reenter chaos, or fight to maintain His peace.

There, lined up on the table, were five symbols of the five stages we see repeated biblically and still today. If water symbolized chaos, that was the senseless shooting. But what has happened since? Is the Spirit hovering; can we see Him? Has God spoken? We knew there wasn't peace that morning, so where were we and what was our role in it all? Passive observers? Charge In-ers? God's kids have been here before, in the midst of stories of chaos. Consider these biblical examples as we discern how to offer ezer-help in a crisis.

First, we see this pattern in the creation account.

- **Chaos**, in the beginning, everything was broken, symbolized by water.
- Then the **hovering Spirit** appeared. "Now the earth was formless and empty, darkness was over the surface of the deep, and the Spirit of God was hovering over the waters" (Genesis 1:2).
- Next, **God spoke** and said a bunch of "Let there bes ..." and the world formed, animals, night and day, water and land.
- His words were powerful, and out of chaos came magnificent order and peace (or **shalom**). "God saw all that he had made, and it was very good" (Genesis 1:31).
- Finally, **temptation** came to Adam and Eve, they sinned, and chaos returned.

Next, we see this pattern in Noah's story.

- **Chaos** is represented by the waters of the flood God sent to wipe out wickedness (Genesis 6–7).
- After forty days and nights on the boat, **the Spirit** came in the form of a dove.
- Then **God spoke:** "Come out of the ark, you and your wife and your sons and their wives. Bring out every kind of living creature that is with you—the birds, the animals, and all the creatures that move along the ground—so they can multiply on the earth and be fruitful and increase in number on it" (Genesis 8:16–17).
- And out of the ark came eight people, saved and redeemed. They were to bring **shalom**, and there was even a rainbow!
- But then Noah **was tempted**, got drunk in his tent, and cursed his son, and the world returned to chaos.

We see this pattern in the story of Moses, who freed God's kids from slavery in Egypt.

- **Chaos** was everywhere. The Israelites were slaves, and their baby boys were being killed in the Nile. "Then Pharaoh gave this order to all his people: 'Every Hebrew boy that is born you must throw into the Nile, but let every girl live'" (Exodus 1:22).
- After the series of plagues got Pharaoh's attention, he let the Israelites go, and **God's presence** divided the sea, leading to their rescue. "Then Moses stretched out his hand over the sea, and all that night the LORD drove the sea back with a strong east wind and turned it into dry land" (Exodus 14:21).
- **God spoke** to Moses and the sea divided. He spoke to Moses and gave the Ten Commandments. He spoke to Moses face to face as one would a friend (Exodus 33).

- The Israelites came out from slavery, and like a birth, there was **shalom**!
- But soon after, they were **tempted**, complained, made a golden calf, and returned to chaos.

In the book of Joshua, we see the pattern again.

- The Jordan River was flooded. We know the presence of water represents **chaos**. "Now the Jordan is at flood stage all during harvest" (Joshua 3:15).
- **God's Spirit** was present, being carried in the Ark of the Covenant.
- **God spoke** and told the priests to get in the water. "And as soon as the priests who carry the ark of the LORD—the Lord of all the earth—set foot in the Jordan, its waters flowing downstream will be cut off and stand up in a heap" (Joshua 3:13). What happened? The river divided.
- Israel was ready to bring **shalom**, to enter the Promised Land.
- But they became **tempted** to take the blessing for themselves and soon attacked Jericho, keeping for themselves what God instructed them to bring to Him. Chaos ensued.

Fast-forward to the ministry of Jesus and imagine the scene depicted in Matthew, where He was baptized.

- No **chaos** was found in Him, but plenty was now in the world. There was the water of the river, and He would enter into that symbolic chaos.
- **The Spirit** came in the form of a dove. "As soon as Jesus was baptized, he went up out of the water. At that moment heaven

was opened, and he saw the Spirit of God descending like a dove and alighting on Him" (Matthew 3:16).

- Then **God spoke**. "And suddenly a voice came from heaven, saying, 'This is My beloved Son, in whom I am well pleased'" (Matthew 3:17 NKJV).
- Jesus came out of the water and **shalom** broke out. The deaf could hear, the blind could see, and the dead were raised to life.
- In the pattern, **temptation** is next, but this time (Matthew 4), it failed and the binding of the evil one began.

The baptism of Jesus is more than Him setting an example *for us* to be baptized. I believe in baptism and the outward declaration of our salvation, but He's also telling the story of what to do when we experience chaos. We enter in, we look for His Spirit, we listen to His voice, we pursue His shalom, and we resist temptation.

In church settings we hear that we can have a relationship with Jesus, and that He wants to guide us, lead us, and love us, but many of us don't experience His personality. We can honor and worship Him and believe He died for our sins, but He's offering us much more than that. He wants us to join Him, and He's teaching us here with His baptism something about His personality: He's a run-to-the-battle kind of Savior. He isn't watching from the banks of the river; He is *all in*. He is introducing Himself to us in the same way a person would, and He'll do it over and again through Scripture (and in life) if we let Him. How much heartache and dysfunction in the Church could be avoided if we paid more attention to emulating His personality than merely following our policies?

Jesus is a run-to-the-battle kind of Savior.

For God's kingdom to grow through us, He must have our obedience. We can't afford to fall into temptation. There's too much at stake! What kind of obedience does He require? More than just "don't swear," "don't envy," or "say nice things to each other." He said when your enemy is hungry, *feed him*. When a soldier asks you to walk a mile, *walk two*. Under Roman law, soldiers had the right to knock on your door and demand a meal at any point, or demand you carry their packs. It's called "angaria," and you couldn't say no. It came to mean any compulsory service or task grudgingly undertaken by the one forced to perform it.

Jesus and His water-entering ways are talking about the kingdom. Give that demanding soldier more than he is asking, then it's service. It gets his attention and gives you, the servant, a chance to put a different kind of kingdom on display. When Jesus came out of the water, He was saying, this time, shalom will come "surely and slowly," but permanently. When Jesus was baptized, His actions announced: I fully accept and commit to bringing shalom to a broken world.

I am a water-enterer.

This was a training moment for the disciples. Jesus was demonstrating "If you want to follow Me, get in the water, enter into chaos." I am heartsick when I hear people say Jesus is boring. Who turned Jesus into something vanilla? A pacifist who pets sheep and looks longingly into the horizon with his flowing locks of hair? Nothing could be further from reality. He loved people with passion, cleared the temple, calmed the raging sea, healed a demon-possessed man ... He was radical, revolutionary, and best of all, knowable.

That Sunday morning, in the company of this hurting church, I confessed to them that it's easy to watch the news and shake our heads, frustrated by a broken world. But God is asking us to enter the water, look for the Spirit, listen for His voice, carry His peace, and resist temptation. Why? Because we love Him. And the more we know Him, the easier it is to love and follow Him. If loving and following are problems, we can't muster up more energy or emotion by "gritting our teeth" and showing up on Sunday mornings. Water-entering is the stuff of ezers. (Adams too, but this isn't a book about them.)

The Church all over the world faces this same decision: what we're willing to do to bring God's presence. We have plenty of examples to follow of biblical, historical, and modern-day chaos-enterers. Biblically, there is Nehemiah, Paul, Daniel, Miriam, Deborah, Esther, Lydia, and Phoebe … they got in the water.

Historically, we have ezers like Katharina Luther, who escaped a convent and became a radical reformer next to her husband, Martin, and Amanda Berry Smith, an itinerant minister who was born a slave and became an evangelist and missionary to Africa.

There's Rosa Parks, who in her book *Quiet Strength* said God helped her the day she refused to give up her seat. "I felt the Lord would give me the strength to endure whatever I had to face. God did away with all my fear. It was time for someone to stand up—or in my case, sit down. I refused to move."[35] She entered into the water and waited for His Spirit to strengthen her.

There are ezers like Sojourner Truth, whose given name was Isabella. She sensed God calling her to change her name to "Sojourner" and travel the country sharing the gospel. Her children were horrified that she thought a poor, illiterate, former slave could survive as an itinerant speaker. Women didn't speak publicly during this time, but Sojourner believed her calling was from God and He would protect her. These chaos-enterers, shalom-bringers are remembered in history not just for their actions but also for their impact. They were bold, vulnerable, and believing.

I just got back from a trip to Israel and was asked by coworkers what stood out for me while I was there. I could've talked about hikes, or insights, or the company I kept while there … but the response came out quickly: *I am returning with steel in my spine.* It comes from the realization I am a part of an old story, with a long family line of water-enterers. There are men and women who went out, sacrificed, spoke up, were martyred, were invited, engaged, and preached. They were unafraid of their circumstances and unencumbered by any consequences. They were watching God's example and following it, and so, now will I.

Besides biblical examples, we have many modern-day ezer water-enterers for inspiration too: Henrietta Mears, Florence Nightingale, Harriet Tubman, and

Corrie ten Boom, whose strong examples and written testimonies shaped my early conviction about what women could accomplish for the kingdom.

Modern-day examples are also women from around the world teaching in classrooms, bringing vulnerable children into their homes, making scientific discoveries, leading movements and organizations, teaching Sunday school, and sharing their faith with hurting neighbors.

Now, with your back straight and your convictions strong, wherever God is calling you to enter the water ...

Go.

Questions to Consider

How do you enter the waters of chaos?

How do you experience Jesus' personality?

What examples or testimonies have shaped what you believe women can accomplish for the kingdom?

Journal

What has entering the waters cost you?

Chapter 25

Are you ready for where He might be sending you?

I was recently seated at a gathering for a woman who had been a missionary in communist Laos for more than forty years. She told me the story of a man who came to know Christ in their ministry and was incarcerated for sharing the gospel. Now his wife sews scripture into the hems of fresh clothes and drops them off on her permitted monthly visits. He commits the passages to memory and shares them with fellow prisoners. When a new convert is released, he directs them to his wife, who disciples and then connects the person to an underground church.

This co-missioning relationship defines the two-plank principle. I tried to imagine being in their position, and the courage someone would need knowing their life was constantly at risk. The most dangerous people in the world are those who are comfortable with imminent death. They exemplify frontline courage.

Christ might not be calling you to risk your life, but is He calling you to more than following Him through church attendance, tithing, and quiet times? Our faith must have a missional component to it, or else it dies in the land of comfort and to-do lists.

Ezer implies engagement: offering help to those who critically need it. Where is He calling you to engage? How can you hear Him? We partner with the work of the Holy Spirit by applying the Word to our lives and paying attention to *kairos* moments. *Kairos* is a Greek word meaning "time," but not the kind of time that *chronos* means. Instead, kairos is a moment in time that is suspended, almost pregnant. In modern-day Christianity, when someone mentions having a "kairos" moment, they are referencing when God got through to them: seemingly stopping time to get their attention.

Ezer implies engagement: offering help to those who critically need it. Where is He calling you to engage?

When my son was about to graduate from high school, I found myself wanting to tell him everything ... to make sure he knew *the most important things* before he left. Things like understanding who you are, taking every opportunity to deepen your faith, and always calling your mother ... There's a passage in Matthew 16 where Jesus knew He didn't have much time left with the disciples, and He was looking for ways to share *the most important things*. He took them on a field trip to Caesarea Philippi, almost twenty-five miles from where they normally spent their time. He had something to say, and what followed was a kairos moment for the disciples. Watching them respond to His Word models how we are to do the same.

> When Jesus came to the region of Caesarea Philippi ... (Matthew 16:13)

They stood at the foot of Mount Hermon, a place known for pagan worship of the Greek fertility gods, including the god Pan. It was a large rock formation with a hole in the middle, where water naturally sprang forth each spring. To entice Pan into action, the people conducted perverse sexual acts. (It's where we get the word *pandemonium*.) When the water flowed, they believed the gods had answered, fertilizing their farmland. The Roman world called this location "the Gates of Hell," and in the pagan mind, it was the gate to the underworld. This rock cliff was also referred to as the "Rock of the Gods" because idols and statues of gods and goddesses were placed in small openings cut into the rock.

When Jesus brought the disciples to the area, they must have been shocked. It was their version of a red-light district, a city of people eagerly knocking on the doors of hell. "When Jesus came to the region of Caesarea Philippi, he asked his disciples, 'Who do people say the Son of Man is?'" (verse 13).

We've already established that a good rabbi asks questions (sometimes when God speaks to us, it's with questions and not answers). Jesus was asking them right there in the middle of that chaos: "Who do people say I am?" Not "What are My principles?" or "What ideas have I been talking to you about?" but *"Who am I?"*

> They replied, "Some say John the Baptist; others say Elijah; and
> still others, Jeremiah or one of the prophets." (verse 14)

Those were good guesses because Elijah and John and Jeremiah were passionate prophets and national reformers who stood up to corruption in their day, like Jesus. They were miracle workers, men who spoke the words of God, like Jesus. They also found God in the wilderness and did unpredictable things, like Jesus.

> "But what about you?" he asked. "Who do you say I am?" (verse 15)

Jesus was pushing the kairos. Standing in this place, He asked, "Who do *you* say I am?" This is the same question He's asking us today—in the chaos we see around us, who do *we* say He is? It's an important question because amid our battlegrounds, in the middle of hard, we must know the answer. We study, learn, and metabolize His truth so that in the moments when life is disorienting, we still know who He is. I don't know what kind of pandemonium you have going on, but there has never been a better time to listen for Him.

> Simon Peter answered, "You are the Messiah, the Son of the living God."
>
> Jesus replied, "Blessed are you, Simon son of Jonah, for this was not revealed to you by flesh and blood, but by my Father in heaven. And I tell you that you are Peter, and on this rock I will build my church, and the gates of Hades will not overcome it." (verses 16–18)

Jesus followed the rabbinic principle of using what was around Him to teach. When He spoke about millstones, He was standing in a town that manufactured millstones. When He talked about birds and flowers, He was in a field. When He talked about fish, He was on the water. Christian tradition debates the meaning of "on this rock." Is Peter the rock? Is the truth the rock? Both those answers ignore the cultural setting of Caesarea Philippi. What if Jesus was saying, "I will build My church right here, *on this rock*, *next* to this chaos, and the gates of hell cannot touch it"?

Like today, gates were defensive structures in the ancient world. By saying the gates of hell would not overcome, He was suggesting the gates were going to be attacked. He was on the offensive. We aren't to hole up in church, hoping the enemy doesn't get us. We are to storm the enemy's strongholds and take ground for the gospel—*in places where His message is most needed.*

By this point, the disciples had been studying with Jesus for years, and now He was commissioning them to attack evil and build the Church. Don't hide: storm the gates of hell. His kairos for them was about "go."

What always amazes me is that God looked at the crew He walked there with and thought this was the best plan. Knowing this message needed to go out into all the world, He picked men and women who were nobody's first choice and gave them this universe-altering assignment: *go*. And He still operates like this. He still sends us out with our botched theology and impure motives and trusts that we can carry our stories in such compelling ways that people unfamiliar with Him will want to know Him.

Jesus continued with this field trip: "I will give you the keys of the kingdom of heaven; whatever you bind on earth will be bound in heaven, and whatever you loose on earth will be loosed in heaven" (verse 19).

He gives us the keys to go on His behalf into hard places. If we want to know what God sounds like ...

> Then Jesus said [in Greek it's "calls," implying He yelled what's next to His disciples], "Whoever wants to be my disciple must deny themselves and take up their cross and follow me. For whoever wants to save their life will lose it, but whoever loses their life for me will find it. What good will it be for someone to gain the whole world, yet forfeit their soul? Or what can anyone give in exchange for their soul? For the Son of Man is going to come in his Father's glory with his angels, and then he will reward each person according to what they have done." (verses 24–27)

In a city filled with false idols, Jesus asked His disciples to commit to one true God. He walked them there to say, "Build My church *here*. Go to the most degenerate places you can find, every red-light district where I am not known, and build My church." I hear that challenge and think, yes, I can stay in a relationship with that someone who is driving me crazy but doesn't know God. Yes, I can take a risk, make a stand, offer a hand. Yes, I can live and give and serve and engage and fight and every other verb you can think of ... yes, I can hear the Jesus challenge and answer *yes*.

The disciples had a kairos moment: they heard the Word and it informed their next steps. He said "Build My church" and that's exactly what they did. They went to the ends of the earth and gave their lives doing exactly what they were told to do by their Rabbi.

Here's what we believed happened next:

- Peter and Paul were both martyred in Rome around AD 66. Paul was beheaded. Peter was crucified upside down at his request, since he did not feel he was worthy to die in the same manner as his Lord.

- Andrew went to the "land of the man-eaters," in what is now Russia and nearby countries. He also preached in Asia Minor, modern-day Turkey, and Greece, where he too was crucified.

- Thomas was most active in the area east of Syria. Tradition has him preaching as far east as India. He died there when pierced through with the spears of four soldiers.

- Philip had a powerful ministry in Carthage in North Africa and then in Asia Minor, where he converted the wife of a Roman proconsul. In retaliation, the proconsul had Philip arrested and cruelly put to death.

- Matthew the tax collector ministered in Persia and Ethiopia. Some of the oldest reports say he was stabbed to death in Ethiopia.

- Bartholomew's missionary travels, by tradition, covered to India back to Armenia, and also to Ethiopia and Southern Arabia. There are various accounts of how he met his death as a martyr.

- James the son of Alpheus ministered in Syria. The Jewish historian Josephus reported he was stoned and then clubbed to death.

- Simon the Zealot ministered in Persia and was killed after refusing to sacrifice to the sun god.
- Matthias was the apostle chosen to replace Judas. Tradition sends him to Syria with Andrew and to death by burning.
- John is the only apostle thought to have died from old age. He led the church in Ephesus and is said to have taken care of Mary the mother of Jesus. An early Latin tradition has him escaping unhurt after being cast into boiling oil in Rome.[36]

When Jesus speaks, we are to act on it. And now we are back to the beginning, when people later asked the disciples the same question Jesus once did, "Who do people say the Son of Man is?" Their lives displayed He is One worth dying for.

Jesus has taken me on His own version of that twenty-five-mile walk, leading me away from the familiar and comfortable to places I didn't plan. I can be sore from that journey. It's work, and part of me would rather not go. Now when life feels "fine" and I feel "fine," I worry. "Fine" is the lullaby of the enemy who whispers to me temptations of comfort. Because it's hard work to walk that far, it's hard work to not join the crazy, it's hard work to stay and engage when running away is easier. Ezer, we were made to hear Him and join Him, not to create lives that are "fine." I hear Him call to me every time I open the Word. And He's asking me, "Who do you say I am?"

It's tempting to only say the stuff we like in response to that question, such as "He's the giver of all good gifts," "He is the forgiver of my sins," "He is the One who promises eternal life" ... and to be sure, those are true and there is a lot I gain in Christ. But the kairos of this passage is: *Am I willing to go, do, give, and serve wherever He says to me?*

Because He also tells me in His Word:

- He is the One who storms the gates of hell. *(Will I follow Him there?)*

- He is the One who offered Himself as the ultimate sacrifice. *(Will I follow His example and lay my life down?)*
- He also made Himself nothing, taking the very nature of a servant. *(Will I be inconvenienced for Him? Sacrifice for Him?)*

The call to help as an ezer is answered in walking, offering, serving, battling, testifying, sacrificing ... those are not the activities of the "fine," but they are the stuff stories are made of.

Amy Carmichael was born in Ireland but lived most of her life as a missionary in southern India. She learned the Tamil language and, initially, was an itinerant evangelist. She led many Indian women to Christ and lived among those who had been persecuted after being converted to Christ from Hinduism. She became aware that many Indian children were dedicated to the Hindu gods by their parents and lived as prostitutes and slaves in the temples. It became her mission to rescue and raise these children, and the Dohnavur Fellowship was born. She first took in girls, and then boys, creating a large hostel and a hospital for children. Eventually, she helped save thousands of children despite constant opposition. As a social reformer, Amy led the movement that saw the law in India changed to protect children from trafficking and prostitution. She saw darkness, but instead of shrinking, she used her mind and hands to engage in war and make a beachhead for light.

Not all testimonies of *yes* sound the same. While some of us storm the gates of hell, others will love children who challenge us, or we will be faithful examples to neighbors who hardly notice. We will serve extended family and be emotionally consistent friends. Faithfulness is not measured in output; it's the inner work of taking thoughts captive, replacing lies with truth, dying to our agenda, and asking the Holy Spirit for wisdom, provision, discernment, and strength. Ezer work is often not sexy, but the results are always the same: *help*. Wherever He takes you, remember you are a suitable helper, an engaged warrior, and a representative of the One who has rescued you.

Questions to Consider

Where has God taken you on a field trip to teach you something?

When was the last time you experienced a kairos moment?

What makes you say no to God?

Journal

Where have you been bold?

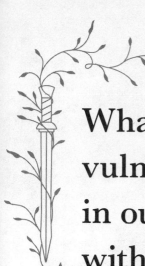

Chapter 26

What role does vulnerability play in our relationship with other ezers?

On a girls' weekend, I was talking with two friends—the deep kind of talking, about what makes us feel seen and also what we tend to hide from others. At first, we discussed hiding our weaknesses from one another, but then I confessed I am more likely to hide my strengths. "I don't want other women to know all I have going on or where I've experienced success. I'm not totally sure why, but I do know that if someone really knows me, it's because I've told them what I've accomplished, not where I've failed."

You can tell when you're speaking a vulnerable truth because the body reacts. Sometimes your breathing gets quicker, your heart beats faster, tears form, or there is a catch in the throat. Honesty exposes us. And sharing with my friends what was going well weirdly made me feel vulnerable. Why is it easier to share a "hard" story or a weakness than it is to share something you're proud of?

That feels vulnerable for me to confess, but I am not alone. One quick Google search of vulnerability studies on women leads to dozens of scholarly articles on this topic. Researchers have tried to discern why in some settings women are intimate supporters of each other, telling their deepest secrets (even more than their romantic partners), while in other settings the competitive spirit of women prevents this kind of camaraderie. How can we vulnerably open up to other women and learn from one another?

Author Brené Brown said, "Vulnerability is the birthplace of love, belonging, joy, courage, empathy, and creativity. It is the source of hope, empathy, accountability, and authenticity. If we want greater clarity in our purpose or deeper and more meaningful spiritual lives, vulnerability is the path."[37] How do we know we are being vulnerable?

Vulnerability is costly, but it's an *exchange*. We are curious about others, we say what we mean, and we put ourselves in a position to be rejected. We show our sense of humor, knowing some won't find us funny. We initiate with people we don't know, or we tell someone what we admire about them. I am done with relationships where there isn't an exchange. I want to hear, learn, grow beside others, and be open to challenge and edification. It's risky, but it's rich.

Vulnerability is costly, but it's an *exchange*.

At a conference I attended, the organizers assigned us to tables with people we didn't know. Only one other woman sat at my table. She was quiet during discussions, but I was curious about what was going on behind her bright eyes. We found each other during the break, and I asked her how she was liking the content. She opened up (demonstrating vulnerability) and told me she had just accepted Christ nine months prior. She was learning so much at this stage and couldn't get enough of her Bible. Then she averted her eyes and tearfully admitted that she felt an almost burning in her soul and didn't know how to talk about it in front of others, because everyone else seemed so calm about their salvation. Her testimony moved me, and when she looked up, she registered surprise that I, too, had tears in my eyes.

"Have you learned about the prophet Jeremiah?" I asked her. "He says something similar in Jeremiah 20:9, 'His word is in my heart like a fire, a fire shut up in my bones. I am weary of holding it in; indeed, I cannot.' I am sorry if it seems the longer we walk with Jesus, the more controlled our faith appears, but that's not how it's designed. If you feel the fire, show off the fire."

The rest of our conversation was about passion, longing, and spiritual hunger. She asked, as I get older, if I struggle with taking risks. She assumed that since more is now on the line (higher stakes), I might be more careful than I once was. "The opposite is true," I answered. "The older I get, the *more* testimony I have of God following through on His promises. I am riskier now because He has a long track record of not letting me down."

She fed off my encouragement, I fed off her joy, and we both walked away inspired—she that spiritual maturity didn't have to mean being careful, me that God is still captivating new children all the time. May we fan the flames of fire in other ezer souls!

It isn't a luxury to ponder these things; ezer is innately worth it. We may think only *some* women deserve to live alive or strong. Or only *some* can be loved or have an adventure or correspond with another. But nothing could be further from the truth! This isn't the right of extra-godly women, older women, beautiful women, special women ... ezer doesn't have to try harder, be better. She can just *be*, as she was created.

I met "Mamá Martha" thirty years ago when she was just starting a children's home. Over the years, I've told her stories on stages, in books, and in groups. I've prayed for and with her, and she's taught me some incredible lessons about provision, persistence, and perspective. Martha is one of those women that when you meet her, you feel drawn not only to what she shows you but what you know lies underneath: layer upon layer of God showing up and building in her a faith in Him that seems relentless. I wanted to peel back some of those layers and ask her how it started for her, what her early ezer days were like.

"I found myself alone late in life," she told me. "And I was drawn to people who needed mercy. I simply wanted to focus on others, and I started in the jails and the slums. I used to stand up in church and tell everyone that on the weekend I was going to this jail or that drug house, and I'd beg people to come with me. But they wouldn't. So, for four or five years, I went mostly alone to minister." (She didn't know it, but I was taking notes. Lesson 1: Follow your calling, regardless of the response.)

"Were you ever in danger or afraid?" I leaned forward, curious.

"I was more afraid of what would happen to me if I stayed home than if I went!" She laughed. "As God would have it, He left me feeling dissatisfied; He gave me a sense there was something else to come. Eventually, He directed me to minister to orphans." (More personal notes. Lesson 2: Obedience is our primary responsibility. We don't need to wait for the approval of others to begin.)

"Did you have people telling you that you should just live out the rest of your retirement in peace? That you deserved it? Earned it?" I asked.

"Oh, yes, most people tried to stop me, though I don't know why. I feel most alive when I am ministering. I think some people just found it too tiring to worry about me," she said. She went on to describe the many challenges she had faced when first opening her children's home: namely land and staff. These were burdens she lifted daily to the Lord. *"If this is what You want ..."* her prayers would always begin. (Lesson 3: Prayer is our greatest source of strength.)

Slowly, the pieces started falling into place. The land was donated, staff appeared, and funding trickled in—just enough to open the doors. She found herself dipping into her savings for many months to balance the books. "But it's all the Lord's money anyway," she insisted. (Lesson 4: Sacrifice is worship.)

Wouldn't it be great if after we made a difficult choice, after we started down a path of God's leading, our affirmation would come in the form of easy days and easy ways? As I listened to Martha talk about her orphanage's beginnings, I wondered if *struggle* were the confirmation of being on the right road and blue skies were actually a warning. I suggested this to Martha, and she replied, "We are in work opposed by the enemy. He doesn't want God glorified in you; He doesn't want light exposing his schemes. He wants you to quit, so yes, the devil will try and use every tool at his disposal to discourage you. You must stand strong." (Lesson 5: Spiritual warfare is a confirmation of the calling.)

Then she smiled as she added, "It's all worth it, though, when I walk out of the office and hear shouts of 'Mamá Martha.'" She was *mamá* to hundreds of children in the thirty years since her home opened its doors. Patiently and quietly, she lifted their eyes from their circumstances, up to a God who has a purpose for every life.

She told me another story: "A couple of years ago, I woke up at 3:00 a.m. feeling a burden for some unpaid bills. I told the Lord, 'I am the servant; You are the King. If You provide for Your work, I will gladly continue, but I cannot muster it up anymore.'" (Lesson 6: We can ask God to be God.) "The next morning, Todd came to tell me of a sponsor who agreed to cover the orphanage's expenses for at least a year. Ever since that day, I wake up at 3:00 a.m. to say a short prayer and remember what the Lord did that night." (Lesson 7: Gratitude is active.)

I drove home after listening to her story and stored up all the truth I had learned from her. There are two storylines always going on, and part of Martha's wisdom is never forgetting about the one we can't see. There's the grocery-store, office-work, recreation life we see building with our eyes, and then there's the otherworldly, angel, demon, eternal life at war with us. Making choices to engage in the world we cannot see gives meaning and mission.

Life offered Martha a path that looked more appealing—less work, pain, stress, and heartache. If she had just quietly lived out her retirement in peace, it would have been socially acceptable and a relief to those around her. But she chose a harder way, and by her testimony, she felt richer, fuller, more satisfied, more loved, and more alive. Who wouldn't want that?

We are constantly advised to take care of ourselves (which is important) and to maintain balance (which has value), but it can be tempting to stop when the Spirit is still saying "Go!" Instead of listening to ourselves and knowing our limitations, shouldn't we listen to the Spirit and heed His direction?

Sometimes that might look like stillness when we want activity. Sometimes that means working when we're tired, listening when we have other plans, or giving up when we'd rather not. If the Bible teaches that God is an ezer to His people, then we can deduce that an ezer represents strength and, like God, an ezer is alert to the needs of others. She isn't self-absorbed, or busy trying to be self-important. She just is. Ezer. Ready to be deployed.

Recently, Martha went home to be with Jesus. In her eighties, she was still praying, working, and learning from God until the end. She honored her calling and gave Him credit for all He did through her. *That's an ezer.* Fighting battles for ourselves, our spouses, our children, our friends, our beliefs, the vulnerable, the marginalized, our neighbors, the unreached ... For the Lord, and not anyone else, we go to war.

Questions to Consider

What is your relationship with vulnerability like?

What does someone have to know about you to know you well?

What is something you felt called to do that others didn't understand?

Journal

Who is someone whose life has taught you many lessons?

Chapter 27

What do the warrior of Eden and the Proverbs 31 woman have in common?

As the mother of a large family, I learned a long time ago, it requires everyone to make the household function well. I used to have a chore chart, but it was met with resistance and *that* was no fun to enforce. Then we rebranded it, and the chore chart was thrown out. The "contribution list" was born, the focus being that everyone has a role in our family instead of a duty to fulfill. I took every opportunity to remind the kids that the house belongs to everyone, and we all need to take care of it.

The contribution list is the key to our happy coexistence. They aren't working for my husband and me when asked to clean a bathroom, fill up a car with gas, or make a meal; they are helping the entire family and we are all accountable to each other and grateful for one another. That's a far cry from begrudging a chore or, worse yet, the person who asked you to do it. If someone ends up doing something extra, that's to their credit, and we are all grateful. It has helped curb resentment and foster maturity.

It took some conversation in our marriage to get here because of our different backgrounds. I grew up in a household where my mother did most of the housework, and I now realize the tasks she taught me were more her way of keeping me busy than actually making a difference in her load. My husband grew up in a household where the kids worked hard, and he often had more responsibilities in the home than were age-appropriate. Finding the middle ground where our children feel responsibility and contribution has been hard-fought but well worth the result.

Watching this all go down in my home made me wonder about my own spiritual maturation and its tie to duty versus responsibility. There is a discipline that comes with a life in Christ. As much as I want to live in the land of grace and rainbows, there is a reality full of sacrificial generosity, taking thoughts captive, and tongue-holding. Those can *feel* like work (even though I know they should come from an overflow of the Holy Spirit in my life).

When I do what is biblically asked of me, I am contributing to the kingdom instead of keeping a list of rules. God sees worth in my participation and wants to partner with me. This makes me feel valuable and puts me on the hunt to look for more opportunities to contribute, instead of crossing off items on a list and rushing to be done.

I resisted the Proverbs 31 woman for a long time, thinking her impossibly high standard was too much of a measuring stick for anyone to come out feeling good about themselves, but over time, I've softened on her. She was just "working with eager hands" and "setting about her work vigorously" (see verses 13, 17). She was hustling and I can respect that. Her open hands to the poor and nonanxious presence (verses 20–21) made her the kind of ezer others felt safe around. She embodied this idea of discipline and contribution and didn't seem too caught up in what she was allowed to do or say or where she was allowed to go or lead. She feared the Lord, looked to Him, and got *after* it.

It's crazy God wants to partner with us as we work; we do our part and He does His. When we do, it's a blessing to others. Both Matthew 5 and 1 Peter 2 talk about others "seeing our good deeds and glorifying God." Work brings glory to Him (1 Corinthians 10:31), is a witness for others (Matthew 5:16), provides for ourselves and those dependent on us (1 Timothy 5:8), and allows for something to share with the needy (Ephesians 4:28). Our work (as unto Him) is a form of worship. When an ezer engages with any kind of work, she uniquely contributes to her household.

The world tells me my value is measured by my position, paycheck, the kind of car I drive, or my house, and we're not sure what to make of work. A little more money will solve all my problems. But a look back at Eden tells me that's not true ... Work began with Adam and Eve and has always had a place in our lives. Once they ate that apple, the blessings given to them through their work became a curse. Now we have two realities, work as a curse and work as a blessing or partnership with God.

Thanks to insights by Dr. Sandra Richter in her brilliant book *Epic of Eden*, I more clearly see the relationship between work and the Genesis curse. In the curse, Eve was told she'd have pain in childbirth. "I will make your pains in childbearing very severe; with painful labor you will give birth to children" (Genesis 3:16). Eve was a life-giver, and now within the curse, the chief cause of her death before the industrial age would be childbirth. Adam's curse was "by the sweat of your face will you have food to eat until you return to the ground" (Genesis 3:19 NLT). "Sweat of your face" is a Near Eastern idiom that represents anxiety perspiration inducing fear. Constant gnawing dread that there will not be enough, that the labor will not meet the need. Richter wrote:

> What if the crop fails? The livestock dies? A fire, storm or drought? Can you relate? What about groceries this week? Rent, mortgage and car payment? College tuition? Retirement? What if I get sick? What if my kids get sick? I am a citizen of the richest nation in the world, I have a secure position at a well-endowed seminary and *still I worry*. And so do you. This is the curse of Adam—limited resources, an insecure future, and a world that no longer responds to my command.[38]

This is our strange start to a relationship with work. How can I get back the sense that the work I do as an ezer is a blessing and partnership? "The LORD God took the man and put him in the Garden of Eden to work it and take care of it" (Genesis 2:15). This is His plan. Which kingdom do I want to live in? The one that says work and money will never be enough? And that my value is in what I *do*? Or one that sees myself as a steward of the work and calling He's given me? And my value is in Whose I am? The latter is the song of an ezer.

Even as we must work, God says our value is not measured by what we earn or do but by who we are: beloved sons and daughters of God. "See what great love the Father has lavished on us, that we should be called children of God!" (1 John 3:1). We work to contribute as one of His kids.

Once when Todd and I were in Israel, we walked the ruins of the temple that Herod built with Jewish laborers. At the time they were used, only the front of the bricks were visible, but now that the building is in ruins, we can see that the back of the stones hold the same craftsmanship as the front. It was as if those workers determined they were going to work for the Lord and not for Herod. God tells us to work wholeheartedly:

> Servants, do what you're told by your earthly masters. And don't just do the minimum that will get you by. Do your best. Work from the heart for your real Master, for God, confident that you'll get paid in full when you come into your inheritance. Keep in mind always that the ultimate Master you're serving is Christ. The sullen servant who does shoddy work will be held responsible. Being a follower of Jesus doesn't cover up bad work. (Colossians 3:23–25 MSG)

Be warned, though, ezers; it's possible to become enslaved to work ...

- When we place our self-worth in work rather than in God (1 John 3:1).
- When we become too concerned with the praise of other people (Matthew 23:5–7).
- When earning becomes our security rather than God (1 Timothy 6:17).

- When we wonder if God wants us as ezers to work more than He wants us to serve. We aren't His employees; we are His children.

Todd and I created a workshop to present at a conference for other orphan-care workers titled "Taking your start-up nonprofit to a mid-sized organization." In our own experience, we went from an organization of two people to one hundred, and our initial budget of twenty thousand dollars swelled to five million. We had *so many* cautionary tales and hard-learned best practices that we wanted to share with other orphan-care organizations.

We made twenty copies of our handouts and prayed for ten unique organizations to come. We opened the door, and over four hundred people walked in. We were just overwhelmed and said, "Whatever we've created—documents, training, policy manuals—you can have. Take our name off it and put your logo on it. If it's only partially what you want, hopefully, it will propel you faster toward your goals."

Within a year, we doubled in size; you can't give away what God's given you without Him blessing it. In Exodus, Isaiah, Malachi, and the Gospels, He talks about work and talents being ours to give away, not hoard. We can't break the spiritual principle: God honors it when we share our work. He wants us to work as a blessing, He wants us to work for His glory and not ours, and He wants us to share the fruit of our work. So now the bigger question is, *where* does He want us to work? Where is the battlefront He's deploying us to?

There are no right answers: how much we should work ... where we should work (marketplace or ministry) ... how we should work (get paid or volunteer, work full-time or part-time). The answers to these questions are uniquely wrapped up in the story God has written for our lives. We miss out on so much when we become transactional with God. All of life is a story, and if we fail to see it that way, we are at risk of thinking the purpose of work is for us to earn 90 percent of what we make while we set aside His 10 percent. His will for us is bound up in the gifts He's given us and the needs of those we carry a responsibility for; trusting work in all its forms can be worship.

Back to the Proverbs 31 woman: as the chapter lists all her résumé-building skills (negotiation, manufacturing, philanthropy, sales), it also testifies to her character:

"She is clothed with strength and dignity; she can laugh at the days to come. She speaks with wisdom, and faithful instruction is on her tongue. She watches over the affairs of her household and does not eat the bread of idleness" (verses 25–27). Could it be God cares more about how we work than what work we do?

As I sit with the Lord and ask Him all my questions regarding the fields I am considering buying or the linen garments I am trying to sell (verses 16, 24), I sense Him prod me more about pride, ambition, and generosity than He does about the direction I am heading or the hours I am working. He has always looked at the heart, while I can be distracted by the direction my feet are pointed or whether I should go five miles per hour or ten. Jesus was a three-miles-per-hour mover, walking everywhere He went. At that pace, there is time to evaluate prospects, assess motives, pray about opportunities, and give Him glory for the work we partner with Him in doing.

Our job isn't results, it's obedience. At Back2Back's twenty-fifth-anniversary party, I said to everyone I was going to try to obey God and let Him count it all up later how He wanted. Anything else would be exhausting. "The LORD is the one who goes ahead of you; He will be with you. He will not fail you or forsake you. Do not fear or be dismayed" (Deuteronomy 31:8 NASB). This promise defeats the inevitable doubt, discouragement, and hopelessness that comes when it doesn't seem our warrioring is making a difference. We ezers must hold fast to our dreams, while understanding the work of *becoming* the kind of warrior God entrusts dreams like ours to.

***

We ezers must hold fast to our dreams, while understanding the work of *becoming* the kind of warrior God entrusts dreams like ours to.

Abigail G. Tomlinson wrote to me on social media:

> Hearing a better interpretation of the word "ezer" has given me so
> much more confidence in my marriage and my relationships with
> others. Life saver, warrior, a powerful term used mainly by God
> when his people desperately need him to come through for them.
> Does that describe what my role is to be in creation and the king-
> dom? Wow. What might my life look like if I lived that out better
> daily? "Helper" doesn't just seem submissive, it feels smaller and
> lower than. Almost like when a mother lets her toddler "help" her
> with cooking dinner, but doesn't expect to receive much actual
> help, but rather an expectation of the child's obedience and learn-
> ing. I think the church would be far mightier even than it is if the
> daughters of Christ understood their roles in it (and in creation
> in general) better.

Questions to Consider

How does work bring meaning to your life?

What is your understanding of work? Curse or blessing? Does it depend on the
task?

If Jesus was a three-miles-per-hour mover, what is your pace in comparison?

Journal

Do you spend more time thinking about how you work or what you work on?

The Blessing

As we've explored in this book, we've never been in a more confusing time regarding gender and roles. New terms and social media bring confusion, op-eds and college courses cause debate (not always constructive), children are hurt, marriages break, and churches split. We are clearly not in a restored creation; we live in an Order of Brokenness. It's the "now, but not yet ..." One day all these questions will be null; we will all be living fully within the design God intended. But today we are stuck in this cracked world with fragmented understanding and wrecked systems.

Since it's our job as Christ followers to reflect the kingdom of heaven on earth, this conversation matters in order to heal what's broken, to unify, and to better show His creation as it was intended.

God never intended for ezer to minimize herself when a man is around, offer only part of herself, or put herself last. We are in a war against an unseen but very real enemy. He wants to ruin us because he knows that hurting us will hurt God, and that's his goal. We need *all* ezers to bring *all* they have to bear—strength, insight, gifts, discernment, experience, wisdom, and prayer. We must keep showing up. If we take women out of the equation, we bench half of the army.

In biblical times, one important practice was giving and receiving a blessing from generation to generation. Fathers and mothers passed along what was given to them: a covenant blessing and promise that made you proud to be in their family, to be called their kid. This was the favor of God and a hopeful future that was transferred generationally.

Below is a blessing from a perfect Father who is crazy about you.

But for twenty-five years, I've worked in hard storylines with broken families, and I know when I bless others with words like "you are God's kid," it can trigger some who don't *like* being someone's kid and who don't understand what it means to *benefit* from being called a child of God. They look at God through the filter of how they saw an earthly parent or assume God talks to us and about us like an unhealthy parent once did.

If you heard words of blessing growing up, tell Jesus thank You. Good people must have told you good truth, and we can live healthier as ezers if someone sowed into us at critical developmental stages. Hear this blessing and allow it to reinforce what you know is true.

If you *didn't* hear words of blessing growing up, God the Father wants to give this blessing to you directly. These are all promises that came from His Word. He recorded these words so we could hear and metabolize them as truth. God thoroughly delights in you.

> *Dear Ezer,*
>
> *I love you. I picked you before the creation of the world. I delight in how you were made: in your personality, your sense of humor, your creativity, your very self.*
>
> *I created you and I honor your life. I bless you in My name and bless all you put your hand to; everything you do, you do for Me.*
>
> *I forgive you. You are reconciled to Me. There is nothing that would separate you from My love. I know everything about you and am crazy about you.*

I redeemed you. I paid the ransom for sin, thinking of you, knowing it was all worth it to be connected for eternity with you. You've been bought with a price and are worth it.

I gift you all you need. Wisdom, patience, peace, joy, discernment, love ... whatever you need, I will provide. You don't need to look anywhere else.

I hear you. I love listening to you share your life with Me. I want to connect with you: in the light and in the dark, in the valley and on the mountaintop. I see you, and My eyes are full of compassion and love.

You are Mine. You are adopted. You are My child, grafted into My tree. I will go to any lengths for you. I will come to you, lift you up, be your Father, and extend mercy toward you. I will go before you and be your rear guard.

You are blessed and gifted. Being My child on this earth comes with privileges, you have grace and peace available to you in abundance.

You are a new creation. The old is gone, the new has come. Walk confidently in My power and enter into every space knowing you bear My name.

You are free from condemnation. Now go, live and love in freedom. Don't let anyone try to whisper to you lies about your identity. You are not what you have done, you are what I have created. I look at you with grace.

You are secure in My hand. So with the authority and power I have, I release a blessing and anointing on you. You are My kid. This means everything. Walk in My way, carry My name, rest in My love, share My heart ... I see you and I love you.

Amen.

Questions to Consider

What part of this blessing means the most to you?

Which part is hard to believe is true?

What do you believe about women now that you didn't before you started this book?

Journal

How will you live differently now?

Acknowledgments

While writing this book, there were days I wavered between bold and nervous. Concerned this message might be misunderstood, I took full advantage of anyone who would hold my hand during the writing process, so there are lots of people to thank.

First, I want to thank the many women who showed me how to be true to how they were made and, simultaneously, true to God. The diversity of godly women in the body of Christ is breathtaking. They work and stay at home, are up front and behind the scenes, are married and single. They are every class, color, and age. I thank all of them. I am rich in friendship and grateful to you on my "front porch ..."

Second, I want to thank my family, both my family of origin and the one Todd and I have created. The insights and questions I raise in this book started as dinner conversations and growing-up wonderings. Thank you for engaging in this with me, hearing my heart, and inoculating me from needing the approval of others. Let's keep opening our Bibles together.

Thank you to the people who helped make the book happen. To Bryan Norman (at Alive Literary Agency), I say it every time and I mean it—being your friend and author makes me feel seen, encouraged, and safe. To Michael Covington, you get credit for encouraging me to put this on paper. I pray it's the blessing you hoped it could be. To Stephanie Bennett, thank you for pushing me to say it better, smarter, and sassier. To Chadd and Jack, and the whole Cook team, it's fun to make Christ-centered resources together for ... today's generations.

To my Back2Back family and to Jenna, books don't just happen, they are shaped by endless conversations and shared experiences. Thank you for adding your gifts and insights onto every page. To my families at Northstar and Vineyard, David and Matt, I practiced these messages in front of you, I ezered beside you and am not the same.

To Todd, somehow, in His mercy, He brought us together, and in His kingdom math, 1 + 1 equals more than 2. I love our story ... and am grateful you are willing for me to share it with others.

Jesus, I pray You are honored here. May our whole lives be acts of worship to You. Thank You for inviting us into the story. Hineni.

Amen.

Notes

1. Victor Hamilton, *The Book of Genesis: Chapters 1–17*, The New International Commentary on the Old Testament (Grand Rapids, MI: William B. Eerdmans, 1990), 175.

2. John and Stasi Eldredge, *Captivating: Unveiling the Mystery of a Woman's Soul*, rev. and exp. ed. (Nashville, TN: Thomas Nelson, 2010), 32.

3. Robert Alter, *Genesis: Translation and Commentary* (New York: W. W. Norton, 1996), 9.

4. Credit to Dr. Dean Nicholas for this original thought.

5. Carmen Joy Imes, "Helper: You Keep Using That Word for Women," *Christianity Today*, August 30, 2022, www.christianitytoday.com/ct/2022/august-web-only/womens-rights-leadership-old-testament-using-word-helper.html?utm_source=CT+Weekly+Newsletter&utm_medium=Newsletter&utm_term=342611&utm_content=10644&utm_campaign=email.

6. Beth Allison Barr, *The Making of Biblical Womanhood: How the Subjugation of Women Became Gospel Truth* (Grand Rapids, MI: Brazos Press, 2021).

7. Josephus, *Antiquities of the Jews* (AD 93).

8. John Polkinghorne, *Theology in the Context of Science* (New Haven, CT: Yale University Press, 2009).

9. Wayne Meeks, *The First Urban Christians: The Social World of the Apostle Paul* (New Haven, CT: Yale University Press, 2003), 75.

10. Margaret Mowczko, "The First-Century Church and the Ministry of Women," *MargMowczko.com* (blog), October 8, 2014, https://margmowczko.com/the-first-century-church-and-the-ministry-of-women/.

11. Tertullian, *On the Soul*, 9.4.

12. Radha Vyas, "What Ancient Italian Churches Tell Us about Women in Ministry," *Christianity Today*, October 17, 2022, www.christianitytoday.com/ct/2022/november/women-ministry -art-italy-early-church-photographs.html?utm_source=CT+Weekly+Newsletter&utm _medium=Newsletter&utm_term=342611&utm_content=11179&utm_campaign=email.

13. Adey Wassink and Michelle Wilson, "One Christ: Men and Women Together in Ministry," Vineyard USA, www.vineyardresources.com, 15.

14. Gregory L. Jantz, "Brain Differences between Genders," *Psychology Today*, February 27, 2014, www.psychologytoday.com/us/blog/hope-relationships/201402/brain-differences-between -genders#:~:text=Male%20brains%20utilize%20nearly%207,specific%20area%20of%20the%20 brain.

15. W. Pakenham Walsh, *Modern Heroes of the Mission Field* (London: Hodder and Stoughton, 1882), 34–35.

16. Jonathan Rourke, "Seven Women's Ministries in the New Testament," 9Marks, December 10, 2019, www.9marks.org/article/seven-womens-ministries-in-the-new-testament/.

17. John Chrysostom, *Epistolam ad Romanos*, homilia 31, 2.

18. Chrysostom, *Epistolam ad Romanos*, quoted in Leonard Swidler, *Biblical Affirmations of Woman* (Philadelphia: Westminster Press, 1979), 295.

19. SWNS, "Amount of Time Americans Spend Staring at Screens Has Skyrocketed during Pandemic," *New York Post*, September 2, 2020, https://nypost.com/2020/09/02/average -americans-time-spent-staring-at-screens-has-skyrocketed-during-pandemic/#.

20. C. S. Lewis, *Prince Caspian*, Chronicles of Narnia (New York: HarperCollins, 1994), 206.

21. Aimee Byrd, *Why Can't We Be Friends? Avoidance Is Not Purity* (Phillipsburg, NJ: P&R, 2018), 34; and Winfree Brisley, "Can't Men and Women Be Friends?," Gospel Coalition, August 9, 2018, www.thegospelcoalition.org/reviews/why-cant-friends/.

22. Frederick Buechner, *Telling the Truth: The Gospel as Tragedy, Comedy, and Fairy Tale* (New York: HarperCollins, 1977), 81.

23. Marianne Williamson, *A Return to Love: Reflections on the Principles of "A Course in Miracles"* (New York: HarperCollins, 1996), 190.

24. John and Stasi Eldredge, *Love and War: Find Your Way to Something Beautiful in Your Marriage* (Colorado Springs: WaterBrook Press, 2009), 37.

25. World Harvest Mission, *Gospel Transformation*, 2nd ed. (Greensboro, NC: New Growth Press, 2011).

26. Robert Bellah, et al., *The Habits of the Heart: Individualism and Commitment in American Life* (Berkeley, CA: University of California Press, 1985), 221.

27. Lois Tverberg, "A Closer Look at the Sabbath Commandment," *Our Rabbi Jesus* (blog), September 25, 2020, https://ourrabbijesus.com/articles/a-surprising-insight-on-the -sabbath-commandment/.

28. "Indoor Air Quality," United States Environmental Protection Agency, accessed August 6, 2023, www.epa.gov/report-environment/indoor-air-quality#note1.

29. Mark Buchanan, *The Rest of God: Restoring Your Soul by Restoring Sabbath* (Nashville, TN: Thomas Nelson, 2006), 90, 98.

30. "Harriet Beecher Stowe," *Christianity Today*, accessed August 6, 2023, www.christianitytoday .com/history/people/musiciansartistsandwriters/harriet-beecher-stowe.html.

31. "Stowe's Global Impact," Harriet Beecher Stowe Center, accessed August 6, 2023, www.harrietbeecherstowecenter.org/harriet-beecher-stowe/her-global-impact/.

32. Karyn Purvis, David R. Cross, and Wendy Lyons Sunshine, *The Connected Child: Bring Hope and Healing to Your Adoptive Child* (New York: McGraw-Hill, 2007), https://child.tcu.edu /wp-content/uploads/2015/06/The-Connected-Child-Chapter-Four.pdf, 48.

33. Bob Dodson, "No Pig Bones!," Acts 242 Study, September 29, 2010, https://acts242study.com /no-pig-bones/.

34. C. S. Lewis, *The Weight of Glory: And Other Addresses* (New York: HarperCollins, 2001), 26.

35. Rosa Parks, *Quiet Strength: The Faith, the Hope, and the Heart of the Woman Who Changed a Nation* (Grand Rapids, MI: Zondervan, 1994), 17–18.

36. Ken Curtis, "What Happened to the Twelve Apostles?," *Christianity Today*, April 28, 2010, www.christianity.com/church/church-history/timeline/1-300/whatever-happened-to-the-twelve -apostles-11629558.html.

37. Brené Brown, *Daring Greatly: How the Courage to Be Vulnerable Transforms the Way We Live, Love, Parent, and Lead* (New York: Avery, 2012), 34, emphasis mine.

38. Sandra Richter, *The Epic of Eden: A Christian Entry into the Old Testament* (Downers Grove, IL: InterVarsity Press, 2008), 111.

Bible Credits